Financial Freedom Roadmap

A Guide to Smart Money Management

Financial Freedom Roadmap

A Guide to Smart Money Management

By

William Lawson

Vij Books

New Delhi (India)

Published by

Vij Books
(*An Imprint of Vij Books India Pvt Ltd*)
(Publishers, Distributors & Importers)
4836/24, 3rd Floor, Ansari Road
Delhi – 110 002
Phone: 91-11-43596460
Mobile: 98110 94883
e-mail: contact@vijpublishing.com
www.vijbooks.in

ISBN: 978-81-19438-68-6 (PB)

Contents

Chapter 1   Introduction to Financial Freedom   1

- What is Financial Freedom?   1
- The Financial Freedom Mindset   5
- Blueprint for Prosperity: Setting Financial Goals   9
- Charting Your Course: Building a Sound Financial Plan   12

Chapter 2   Mastering Debt Management   17

- Decoding Debt: Navigating the Complexities of Borrowing   17
- Strategic Debt Repayment: Key Concepts for Financial Well-Being   20
- Streamlining Debt: The Benefits of Consolidation and Refinancing   23

Chapter 3   Building Wealth Through Property   28

- Navigating the Real Estate Market: A Path to Property Wealth   28
- Stepping into Ownership: A Guide to Buying Your First Property   31
- Strategic Pathways: Exploring Real Estate Investment Strategies   35
- Enhancing Wealth: Strategies for Maximising Property Value   39

Chapter 4   Investing for Wealth   43

• Introduction   43

• Foundations of Prosperity: The Basics of Investing   46

• Crafting a Robust Investment Portfolio: Strategies for Success   50

• Strategies for Enduring Wealth: Long-Term Investment Approaches   55

• On Guard for Success: Keeping Your Portfolio in Tune   59

Chapter 5   Securing Tomorrow: Planning for Retirement   64

• Introduction   64

• Securing the Future: The Vital Role of Retirement Planning   70

• Unlocking Retirement: A Guide to Retirement Accounts   73

• Crafting Your Future: Building a Robust Retirement Savings Plan   77

• Boosting Your Future: Strategies for Maximising Retirement Contributions   81

Chapter 6   Navigating Financial Roadblocks   85

• Introduction   85

• Overcoming Financial Hurdles: Strategies for Common Challenges   88

• Financial Safeguard: The Importance of Building an Emergency Fund   92

• Shielding Your Finances: The Role of Insurance and Protection   96

- Planning for the Future: Essential Steps in Legal and Estate Planning — 100

Chapter 7   Social Financing and Community Support — 103

- Empowering Communities: The Role of Social Financing and Support — 103
- Harnessing Finance for Good: Understanding Social Financing — 107
- Harnessing Local Strength: Leveraging Community Resources for Financial Stability — 111
- The Power of Giving: Embracing Philanthropy and Corporate Social Responsibility — 116
- Investing with Purpose: The Essentials of Sustainable and Ethical Investing — 120

Chapter 8   Maintaining Financial Freedom — 126

- Sustaining Prosperity: Strategies for Maintaining Financial Freedom — 126
- Knowledge is Wealth: The Importance of Ongoing Financial Education — 130
- Being Agile in Your Financial Plan Adjustments — 136
- Why you need to adjust your financial plan regularly — 136
- Enduring Wealth: Crafting a Lasting Legacy — 144

Conclusion — 149

- Sustaining Your Financial Freedom — 149

Chapter 1

Introduction to Financial Freedom

What is Financial Freedom?

Financial Freedom is a term that really resonates with a universal aspiration: leading life without worrying about one's finances. It is the state at which an individual has adequate amounts of money to live the type of life they desire without worrying so much about money issues. The spirit of financial freedom, adequacy in resources, and desired lifestyle provide for an aspect of the mindset that needs to be fostered and cultivated and strategic planning that needs to be deployed to ascend along this cherished aspiration.

At the core of financial freedom is feeling in control of your finances rather than having them control you. Basically, financial freedom can be defined as having the ability to make choices in one's life and still being in a position to lead their life relatively free of the stress that comes with money issues. For this reason, one can pursue their passions, enjoy the company of others, travel, and live life at a higher quality. However, financial freedom is not a coincidence; it needs a person to have a deep understanding of personal finances, a disciplined approach toward money management, and a strategic plan developed according to these individual goals.

The process of moving toward financial freedom commences with a sound understanding of what it actually means. An individual has achieved enough wealth that, even if their assets stop generating income, they will have enough to live off for the rest of their life. This financial freedom can be attained in many ways, including the saving, investing, and prudent management of one's expenses. There is really not much to say about the need for financial freedom except to describe it in terms of security and peace of mind, that you can handle emergencies, retire comfortably, or support your loved ones without a financial strain.

Being financially free requires a certain mindset toward growth, learning, and adaptability. This attitude is a reflection of the thirst for financial knowledge and readiness to challenge and change the beliefs that restrict money. Many people are raised with the principles of wrong beliefs about wealth and financial success; they tend to view money as a source of stress and tough life; and, financial independence is not supposed to be theirs. The growth mindset changes this perception that making money and improving one's financial stature is a matter of picking know-how and degree of willingness to go for it.

Financial literacy sets the foundation of the financial freedom mindset. Financial literacy is the possession of the set of knowledge, skills, habits, and strategies that enable an individual to make effective and informed decisions in responding towards issues from day-to-day spending and budgeting to making long-term investments and financial planning. Financially literate individuals are better placed to avoid the pitfalls of personal finance, make significant decisions in avoiding personal finance pitfalls, and seize opportunities of enhanced financial well-being. Ongoing learning and being informed of financial trends is important to maintain and enhance your financial acumen.

Setting clear and attainable financial goals is another critical step toward your financial freedom. Goals provide direction and motivation, helping you stay focused on what matters most. That is the reason there has to be a distinction between short-term and long-term goals. Short-term and long-term goals. Short-term winning goals can include paying off a creeping credit card debt or building an emergency fund, while long term winning goals can take the form of saving for retirement or purchasing a home. The SMART framework ensures that your goals are realistic and within reach, providing a clear roadmap for your financial journey.

Illustration of the whole-solution financial plan is critical towards the translation of one's financial goals to practical steps. A financial plan is simply a report on your current financial position, the goals you want to achieve, and how you will reach them. A financial plan comprises the budget, saving plan, investing plan, and paying off debt. A designed financial plan in the right way is your path to achieving financial independence with the needed flexibility to implement it according to goal variations.

The most typical first step in financial planning would be to figure out your current financial situation. This would involve checking out available sources of income and your expenses, assets, and liabilities. Knowing where you are financially is the basis you need to be able to make decisions wisely about your future. When your picture about your financial status is cleared up, you can start setting realistic and achievable goals.

Planning your expenses and savings is the most fundamental thing in financial planning. The creation of a detailed plan for spending and saving is called "budgeting." In other words, it is an essential tool in financial management. A good budget helps you to live within your means, but also enhances your ability to meet long-term financial goals. Some ways to budget include zero-based budgeting, where every dollar is assigned a purpose, and the 50/30/20 rule, where 50% is allocated to needs, 30% is allocated to wants, and 20% is allocated to savings and debt repayment. Most importantly, remaining disciplined in your approach to budgeting is crucial.

Saving and investing are the most crucial part of the financial plan; therefore, it comes next in the process. Saving is setting aside money for future needs or emergencies, while investment is putting the money to work to increase its overall value over time. A good savings plan accounts for holding an emergency fund for such things, but also an account for a specific goal, such as a down payment toward a house. Investing, on the other hand, is about putting your money into investments such as stocks, bonds, or real estate, to increase your money over time. Knowledge and diversification of your investments are basically very important in building a resilient portfolio and thus understanding the risks and returns very important in financial planning.

Debt can be the biggest hindrance to financial freedom, if well not mitigated. Management of the resources you have borrowed begins with identifying the kinds of debt you have. Then, you give priority to the high-interest one and either pay it off gradually or have an effective debt payoff plan. Other expressions include the debt snowball, which is paying off the smaller debts first, while the debt avalanche argues that you should pay off the high-interest debts first. To ensure this health in financial matters, you must stay away from incurring debt in the future through smart borrowing practices, build emergency savings to cater for unexpected expenses, and, through debt management strategies, ensure you do not expose your assets to creditors. This also means being aware enough to review and make changes to your financial plan as required to ensure you are properly aligned with the end goal of financial freedom.

As previously explained, financial freedom is a multifaceted effort that calls for robust planning, personal finance, strategy nurturing, and financial blueprints. Learn how to develop a growth mindset by setting clear-cut goals and building a strong financial plan. Take charge of your finances and gain freedom to live your way by developing a growth mindset, setting clear goals, and building a financial plan. This is a first chapter toward building experience and tools that will take us closer to our journey toward financial independence and security.

The Financial Freedom Mindset

Achieving financial freedom requires more than just a sound understanding of economics and finance. It necessitates a fundamental shift in mindset. This shift involves cultivating attitudes and habits that support both financial health and long-term prosperity. The financial freedom mindset is characterised by proactive and positive thinking about money, a willingness to learn, and an openness to change. It is about transforming the way we view and interact with our finances, thereby paving the way to a life of financial security and independence.

At the core of the financial freedom mindset lies the concept of a growth mindset. Coined by psychologist Carol Dweck, a growth mindset is the belief that abilities and intelligence can be developed through dedication, hard work, and continuous learning. This stands in stark contrast to a fixed mindset, which assumes that abilities are static and unchangeable. In the context of personal finance, a growth mindset encourages individuals to view financial challenges not as insurmountable obstacles but as opportunities to learn, grow, and improve.

A growth mindset is crucial for overcoming financial challenges and seizing opportunities. It fosters resilience and adaptability—essential traits for navigating the complexities of personal finance. Individuals with a growth mindset are more likely to embrace financial education, seek out new knowledge, and apply what they learn to improve their financial situation. They are proactive in managing their finances, constantly looking for ways to optimise their budgets, increase their savings, and invest wisely. This proactive approach is fundamental to achieving and maintaining financial freedom.

To develop a growth mindset, it is important to embrace financial education actively. Financial education involves understanding the basics of personal finance, such as budgeting, saving, investing, and managing debt. It also includes staying informed about economic trends and financial products. This can be achieved through various means, such as reading books on personal finance, attending financial workshops and seminars, and following reputable financial news sources. Additionally, being open to new financial strategies and willing to adapt your approach based on what you learn can significantly improve your financial health. Engaging with a financial advisor or joining a financial literacy group can also provide valuable support and further your financial education.

Overcoming limiting beliefs about money is another essential aspect of the financial freedom mindset. Many individuals hold deep-seated beliefs that hinder their financial progress, such as "I'm not good with money," "I'll never be rich," or "Money is the root of all evil." These beliefs create psychological barriers that prevent individuals from taking the necessary steps to improve their financial situation. Identifying and challenging these limiting beliefs is crucial for fostering a more positive and empowered approach to financial management.

To overcome limiting beliefs, start by recognising them and understanding their origins. Often, these beliefs are ingrained from childhood or past experiences and may not be based on current reality. Once identified, challenge these beliefs by seeking evidence to the contrary and reframing your thinking. For instance, if you believe that you are not good with money, remind yourself of instances where you made sound financial decisions and focus on building your financial skills. Affirmations and positive self-talk can also help in reshaping your beliefs about money. Surrounding yourself with financially savvy individuals and mentors can provide positive influences and reinforce your new, empowered mindset.

The role of financial literacy in achieving financial freedom cannot be overstated. Financial literacy involves understanding financial concepts, tools, and resources, enabling individuals to make informed decisions about their money. It encompasses a wide range of knowledge, from budgeting and saving to investing and managing debt. Financially literate individuals are better equipped to navigate the complexities of the financial world, avoid common pitfalls, and seize opportunities that enhance their financial well-being.

A strong foundation in financial literacy begins with understanding basic financial concepts. This includes knowing how to create and stick to a budget, the importance of an emergency fund, the principles of saving and investing, and the impact of interest rates on loans and credit. Advanced financial literacy involves understanding more complex topics such as investment strategies, tax planning, and retirement planning. Continuous learning is vital, as the financial landscape is constantly evolving with new products, regulations, and economic conditions.

Staying updated on financial trends and best practices is essential for maintaining and enhancing financial literacy. This can be achieved through various means, such as reading financial news, following reputable financial blogs, participating in financial forums, and attending educational seminars. Engaging with professional financial advisors and planners can also provide valuable insights and personalised advice. By making financial education a lifelong endeavour, individuals can adapt to changes and make decisions that support their long-term financial goals.

In addition to acquiring knowledge, applying what you learn is critical for achieving financial freedom. Practical application solidifies understanding and builds financial competence. Start by implementing basic financial principles in your daily life, such as tracking expenses, setting financial goals, and creating a budget. Gradually incorporate more advanced strategies, such as investing in the stock market or real estate, diversifying your portfolio, and planning for retirement. Regularly review and adjust your financial plan to ensure it remains aligned with your goals and circumstances.

The financial freedom mindset is a transformative approach that empowers individuals to take control of their financial future. By developing a growth mindset, overcoming limiting beliefs, and prioritising financial literacy, anyone can achieve financial independence and enjoy the benefits of financial freedom. This mindset fosters resilience, adaptability, and informed decision-making, all of which are essential for navigating the complexities of personal finance. Embracing these principles will set you on a path to not only achieving financial freedom but also sustaining it throughout your life.

In essence, the financial freedom mindset is about more than just managing money—it is about transforming your relationship with money. It involves cultivating a proactive and positive approach to personal finance, constantly seeking opportunities for growth and improvement, and committing to lifelong financial education. With the right mindset, financial freedom is not just a distant dream but an achievable reality that can bring lasting peace, security, and prosperity.

Blueprint for Prosperity: Setting Financial Goals

Setting goals is a basic and important step to financial freedom. Goals give a person a sense of direction and motivation, directing their efforts and resources effectively. They act as benchmarks of progress and guiding light in making financial decisions. Without clearly defined objectives, the management of finances can be an aimless and reactive process. Formulating financial goals is not the point at which you decide what you want to do, but how you will do it and how you will measure the accomplishment.

A key distinction to make in financial planning is that between a short-term goal and a long-term goal. Short-term goals are usually attainable within a year's time. Examples of short-term goals are establishing an emergency fund, paying off minor debt, or saving toward holiday expenses. Short-term goals are important because they lay the foundation of security and cause a person to feel a sense of immediate accomplishment. For example, if you set a goal to save £1,000 in six months for an emergency fund, just seeing £1,000 in your bank account can make you feel good and secure.

Long-term goals cover a range of years, perhaps the better part of a lifetime, with such major life events as purchasing a home, educating dependent children, or retiring in comfort. Long-term goals require you to work more diligently and strategically. Long-term goals are important because they shape long-term financial health and accomplish major personal objectives. For example, if you set a goal to save £500,000 over 30 years for retirement, you need an aggressive investment strategy and the self-discipline to make regular contributions. Long-term goals are important to have because they help to maintain long-term financial health and can achieve major personal objectives.

The SMART framework is a good tool to set financially clear, realistic, and trackable set of goals. SMART is an acronym for specific, measurable, achievable, relevant, and time-bound. This approach will make sure the goals are well-defined and hence increase the probability of reaching them. Using the SMART criteria in financial goals translates vague aspirations into specific plans. For example, look at the difference between an unmeasurable goal like "save more money" and one that's SMART: "Save £200 per month for the next year, so that by this time next year I will have £2,400 in an emergency fund." This goal is specific (saving a set amount each month), measurable (amount saved can be tracked), attainable (based on current income and expenses), relevant (important for financial security), and time-bound (to be achieved within a year). Again, a long-term goal may be, for example, "Invest £300 a month in a diversified portfolio to accumulate £100,000 for a down payment on a house in 10 years." This approach provides clarity and structure, making it easier to stay focused and motivated.

The prioritization of financial goals is important since resources are limited, and most of these goals may be competing for attention in the list. Such an exercise involves a closer look at the level of urgency, importance, and feasibility of these goals. Rather, it involves proper reflection on personal circumstances, values, and timelines. There is a handful of good strategies, one of which is classifying goals as either needs or wants: Needs, such as paying off high-interest debt or building an emergency fund, should trump goals such as saving for a luxury item.

It might be difficult to juggle multiple goals. For instance, you may need to save for retirement, pay off debt, and save for education – all at the same time. In this case, you will need a balanced approach. Start with those goals that are immediate, high-priority, and will affect your finances quickly, such as repayment of high-interest debt. At the same time, your income flows should be sent towards the long-term aspect, such as saving for retirement, in order that you do not lag behind in these critical areas. A proportional approach to allocation among goals will help you address numerous goals at the same time. For example, you may budget 50% of your savings for debt repayment, 30% for retirement, and 20% for education.

Regular review and tracking of financial goals is important to keep the momentum going and make the necessary course corrections. Financial goals are not sacrosanct; they are to be changed in line with the income, expenses, and life situation. Frequent reviews give you the opportunity to ensure that you are on the right track and moving ahead in the right direction. Tracking of progress can be done with the help of several tools and techniques, such as budgeting apps. In this fashion, it is much easier to know if you are keeping to your financial plan. Keeping a financial journal is even a more personalized way, as you are able to record and reflect on your financial decisions and their consequences. Financial reviews of the period can be made monthly or quarterly and will be a period of checking progress, celebrations of milestones, or even adjustments of goals if need be. All such reviews must encompass all aspects of personal finance, starting from cash accumulation and saving, investing, and even borrowing.

The process of setting financial goals is a dynamic one and calls for careful planning, disciplined execution, and constant monitoring. By establishing their strong financial roadmap—distinguishing between long-and short-term goals, applying the SMART criteria, prioritizing on the basis of individual circumstances and values, and reviewing progress on a regular basis—the road map will navigate daily financial decisions and ensure that long-term aspirations are achievable.

Setting financial goals basically turns wishes into a course of action that in return gives one direction on the clear path towards financial freedom. It catalyzes an individual to be the master of their financial destiny by making prudent choices, resulting in living a life of total security and prosperity. With goals clearly outlined and a strategy in place, financial freedom is no more a distant dream but an achievable goal. But more so, by sticking to the process, you can reach financial stability, security, and, in the final analysis, freedom to live life on your own terms.

Charting Your Course: Building a Sound Financial Plan

A financial plan is more than just a list of financial goals; it's a detailed roadmap that outlines the steps needed to achieve those goals. This comprehensive plan includes budgeting, saving, investing, and managing debt, providing a structured approach to personal finance. A well-crafted financial plan is dynamic, adjusting to changes in circumstances and goals to ensure ongoing financial health and progress.

Every financial plan begins with a thorough assessment of your current financial situation. This involves taking a detailed inventory of your income, expenses, assets, and liabilities. Understanding your financial baseline is crucial for setting realistic goals and developing an effective strategy. Start by listing all sources of income, including salaries, bonuses, investments, and other earnings. Then, document all expenses, categorizing them into essential and non-essential spending. Essential expenses include housing, utilities, groceries, and transportation, while non-essential expenses cover discretionary spending such as dining out, entertainment, and travel. Additionally, compile a list of all assets, such as savings accounts, investments, real estate, and valuable possessions. Finally, detail all liabilities, including mortgages, student loans, credit card debt, and other obligations. This comprehensive assessment provides a clear picture of your financial health and serves as the foundation for your financial plan.

Budgeting is a critical component of financial planning, serving as the framework for managing income and expenses. A well-structured budget ensures that you allocate resources effectively, prioritize essential spending, and save for future goals. Creating a realistic and effective budget requires a detailed understanding of your financial situation and a commitment to financial discipline. One popular budgeting method is zero-based budgeting, which involves allocating every pound of income to specific expenses, savings, or debt repayments, ensuring that your income minus your expenses equals zero. This method encourages mindful spending and helps identify areas where you can cut costs or increase savings. Another widely used approach is the 50/30/20 rule, which allocates 50% of your income to needs, 30% to wants, and 20% to savings and debt repayment. This flexible method provides a balanced approach to budgeting, allowing for both essential and discretionary spending while prioritizing savings and debt management.

Saving and investing are integral to a robust financial plan, addressing both short-term needs and long-term goals. Saving involves setting aside money for immediate and future needs, such as an emergency fund, major expenses, and retirement. Different types of savings accounts, such as high-yield savings accounts, money market accounts, and certificates of deposit, offer varying levels of accessibility and interest rates, catering to different saving objectives. Building an emergency fund is a top priority, providing a financial cushion to cover unexpected expenses such as medical bills, car repairs, or job loss. Financial experts typically recommend saving three to six months' worth of living expenses in an easily accessible account.

Investing, on the other hand, focuses on long-term growth, using your money to generate returns over time. Investment options include stocks, bonds, mutual funds, and real estate, each offering different levels of risk and return. Diversification, the practice of spreading investments across various asset classes, is crucial for managing risk and maximizing returns. For example, a diversified portfolio might include a mix of stocks for growth potential, bonds for stability, and real estate for income generation. Regularly contributing to retirement accounts, such as a 401(k) or Individual Retirement Account (IRA), is also essential for long-term financial security. Understanding the benefits and risks associated with different investment options enables you to make informed decisions that align with your financial goals.

Effective debt management is another crucial element of a successful financial plan. Debt can significantly impact your financial health, limiting your ability to save and invest. Managing debt involves understanding the types and terms of your debt, prioritizing high-interest debt, and developing strategies for repayment. Two popular methods for paying off debt are the snowball and avalanche methods. The snowball method focuses on paying off the smallest debts first, providing a psychological boost as you eliminate debts one by one. The avalanche method, on the other hand, targets the highest-interest debts first, saving money on interest payments over time. Both methods have their advantages, and the choice depends on your financial situation and personal preferences. Additionally, adopting smart borrowing practices, such as avoiding unnecessary debt and seeking the best terms for loans and credit, helps prevent future debt accumulation and supports long-term financial health.

Regularly reviewing and adjusting your financial plan is essential to ensure it remains aligned with changing goals and circumstances. Life events such as job changes, family additions, market fluctuations, and unexpected expenses can impact your financial situation and necessitate adjustments to your plan. Regular reviews, whether monthly, quarterly, or annually, allow you to assess your progress, identify any deviations from the plan, and make necessary adjustments. This ongoing process ensures that your financial plan continues to reflect your current needs and long-term objectives.

Adapting your financial plan in response to major life events is crucial for maintaining financial stability. For instance, a job change might require adjustments to your budget and savings strategy, while starting a family might necessitate increased savings for education and future expenses. Market fluctuations can impact the value of your investments, making it important to review and adjust your investment strategy accordingly. By staying proactive and responsive to changes, you can ensure that your financial plan remains robust and effective.

Building a financial plan is a dynamic and ongoing process that requires careful planning, disciplined execution, and continuous monitoring. By assessing your current financial situation, creating a realistic budget, saving and investing wisely, managing debt effectively, and regularly reviewing and adjusting your plan, you can achieve financial stability and progress towards your long-term goals. This comprehensive approach empowers you to take control of your financial future, providing the security and freedom to live life on your terms. With a well-crafted financial plan, you can navigate the complexities of personal finance with confidence, ensuring a prosperous and secure future.

Chapter 2

Mastering Debt Management

Decoding Debt: Navigating the Complexities of Borrowing

Debt is a complex financial tool that plays a vital role in both personal and business finance. It helps individuals purchase homes, invest in education, and manage cash flow. However, debt also carries risks that can lead to financial distress if not managed properly. Understanding the different types of debt is crucial for effective debt management and making informed borrowing decisions. Each type of debt has its own characteristics and implications, which influence how it should be used and managed.

Secured debt is backed by collateral, which provides security to the lender by ensuring they can recover their funds if the borrower defaults. Common examples of secured debt include mortgages and auto loans. The primary advantage of secured debt is that it usually comes with lower interest rates compared to unsecured debt because the lender's risk is mitigated by the collateral, which can be seized and sold to repay the loan. For instance, a mortgage is secured by the property being purchased, while an auto loan is secured by the vehicle. However, the risk to the borrower is significant. If they are unable to repay the loan, they risk losing the collateral, which could mean losing their home or car. Therefore, while secured debt can be a cost-effective borrowing option, it requires careful consideration and a clear plan for repayment to avoid the severe consequences of default.

Unsecured debt, on the other hand, is not backed by collateral. Credit cards, personal loans, and student loans fall into this category. Because the lender assumes more risk with unsecured debt, the interest rates are typically higher than those for secured debt. Borrowers need to demonstrate strong creditworthiness to obtain favorable terms on unsecured debt. This type of debt can be useful for covering a wide range of expenses, from everyday purchases to consolidating higher-interest debts. However, the absence of collateral means that lenders rely heavily on the borrower's credit history and income stability when assessing risk. Effective management of unsecured debt involves understanding the terms of the loan, such as interest rates, repayment schedules, and any potential penalties for late payments. Prioritizing timely payments is crucial to avoid penalties and high-interest accrual, which can quickly escalate and lead to financial strain.

Revolving debt is characterized by its flexibility. This type of debt allows borrowers to use credit up to a predetermined limit, repay it, and borrow again as needed. Credit cards and lines of credit are common examples of revolving debt. The primary benefit of revolving debt is its flexibility, making it a convenient tool for managing cash flow and unexpected expenses. Borrowers can use the credit as needed and repay it over time, which provides a cushion for financial emergencies. However, this flexibility comes with its own set of challenges. Revolving debt often carries higher interest rates compared to other types of debt, and the interest compounds quickly if balances are not paid off in full each month. This can lead to a debt spiral, where the borrower continues to accrue interest and fees, making it increasingly difficult to pay down the principal balance. Disciplined management of revolving debt is essential to avoid excessive interest charges and potential financial hardship.

Installment debt involves borrowing a fixed amount of money and repaying it in regular installments over a specified period. Mortgages, auto loans, and personal loans are typical examples of installment debt. This type of debt provides predictability in budgeting, as borrowers know the exact amount to be paid each month, which helps in financial planning. The fixed repayment schedule of installment debt can also be reassuring, as it allows borrowers to plan their finances around the repayment obligations. However, the key to managing installment debt effectively is ensuring that the repayment terms are sustainable within the borrower's budget. Taking on installment debt that stretches one's finances too thin can lead to missed payments and financial stress. It is important to carefully consider the terms of the loan, including the interest rate, repayment period, and total cost of borrowing, before committing to an installment debt agreement.

Understanding these different types of debt and their implications is fundamental to effective debt management. Each type of debt serves different financial needs and carries distinct risks and benefits. For instance, while secured debt might offer lower interest rates, the risk of losing collateral can be significant. Conversely, unsecured debt, while not risking personal assets, often comes with higher interest rates and requires a strong credit profile to secure favorable terms. Revolving debt provides flexibility but demands disciplined repayment to avoid high interest costs. Installment debt offers predictability but requires careful planning to ensure the repayment terms are manageable.

A comprehensive approach to debt management involves assessing one's financial situation and choosing the type of debt that aligns best with their financial goals and capacity. This includes considering factors such as the purpose of the loan, the interest rate, repayment terms, and the potential risks involved. Additionally, maintaining a good credit score is crucial, as it affects the terms and availability of both secured and unsecured loans. Regularly monitoring one's credit report, managing existing debts responsibly, and avoiding unnecessary borrowing are key practices for maintaining financial health.

In conclusion, debt is an integral part of modern financial life, enabling individuals and businesses to achieve their goals and manage cash flow effectively. However, it requires careful management and a thorough understanding of its various forms to avoid the pitfalls that can lead to financial distress. By understanding the characteristics and implications of different types of debt, borrowers can make informed decisions that support their financial wellbeing and long-term prosperity.

Strategic Debt Repayment: Key Concepts for Financial Well-Being

Repaying debt is a strategic process that should take place in a manner that assures ongoing, sustainable success and avoids being overwhelmed. Effective debt management includes strategic repayment that optimizes financial pay-off as well as psychological pay-off. Two of the most popular methods include the debt snowball and the debt avalanche. These methods are distinctly different, and the choice of method can depend on individual needs and preferences. A hybrid of these methods may also represent a workable strategy for debt relief.

The primary theory behind the debt snowball method is to start with the smallest debts and make minimum payments on all other debts. The foundation of this method is based on the psychological gains that come from paying off the small debts sooner. The rapidity of paying off the smallest debt enables an individual to reach a payoff stage very quickly in the repayment process. This small quick win is strongly motivational and offers encouragement, enabling the individual to approach larger debts with increased confidence and commitment. When that smallest debt is paid in full, that payment amount is then added to the next smallest debt. This results in an ongoing snowballing effect and will speed up the repayment of the following debts.

The major advantage of the debt snowball is its psychological benefits. These small victories that come when little debts are paid off can be truly empowering and can build momentum that is critical to staying the course over time. It works well in making them feel those small victories while paying back their debt. It should be appreciated for the snowball method may not be the most efficient from a financial point since it does not take into consideration the interest rates of the debts.

Instead, the avalanche method starts with debts having the most expensive interest rates and clears out small debts. The advantage that goes extent into reducing much of the payable interest over time to result in a quick overall debt repayment period. The method of minimizing the amount of time and interest in money paid to service the debts results in saving more money over time. This is an effective method for someone to be driven on the quantitative front since there is no care about the emotional benefits in terms of erasing the smaller debts at the moment.

While the avalanche method takes quite some time into realizing the visual progression when compared to the snowball method, the savings in terms of finances are quite big. By concentrating on high-interest debts, addicts will put themselves in a better position of saving much more money that would be lost to interest payment, thus more savings over time. This is the best approach for people with the discipline to follow through their plan, even though they will not have their more frequent milestones during the earlier stages.

For the others, the Hybrid approach can be their best shot since it holds the strengths of the snowball and avalanche methods in the recommended manner. One can start by identifying a high-interest debt that also has a relatively low balance. For instance, by first paying off this debt, they are able to gain psychologically from having done away with a debt right away and are able to make a financially efficient decision by taking away money from high-interest debt. Once a first debt is paid off, the individual can continue to use the snowball method or else shift to the avalanche method, should that suit their financial situation or personal preferences.

A hybrid approach therefore balances psychological and financial aspects of debt reduction. This can enable people to devise a repayment plan most suitable to their needs and motivations so that success in the long run is maximized. For instance, you may have several high-interest debts, so you pay off the smallest high-interest debt first in order to have a quick win and then switch to the avalanche method of attacking larger high-interest debts. This flexibility can make the debt repayment process more manageable and sustainable.

The real solution to debt payoff, however, is found in being consistent and committed and, of course, it has to go hand in hand with periodic reviews and hence adjustments of the plan to realign it with one's financial goals or changing circumstances. This may include paying more when money is available, negotiating with all creditors for lowering interest rates, and making strides towards increasing income sources to pay down debt faster.

What is more, there is a need to set up a good foundation for personal finance to prevent one from falling back into debt, and this might include putting together an emergency fund, living within one's means, and having a budget that gives priority to saving and reducing debt. Through the application of sound financial practices, these individuals will avoid the pitfalls of debt and really find lasting financial stability.

In layman's words, the debt repayment scheme should be strategic and individualized based on the motivations and needs of the debtor. The first method, the debt snowball, carries psychology advantages, while the debt avalanche method carries financial efficiency through a reduction in the cumulative interest cost. Perhaps a hybrid approach may be the way to maximize the strengths of each method so as to bestow upon the individual a balanced path to debt freedom. In the end, going down a well-structured repayment plan, along with the practice of good financial habits, one can successfully be on the journey to becoming financially healthy and independent.

Streamlining Debt: The Benefits of Consolidation and Refinancing

Debt consolidation and refinancing are powerful financial tools designed to simplify debt management and potentially reduce interest rates, making repayment more manageable and efficient. These strategies can significantly ease the burden of debt, especially for individuals dealing with multiple high-interest obligations. By understanding and properly utilizing debt consolidation and refinancing, borrowers can achieve greater financial stability and progress toward their long-term financial goals.

Debt Consolidation

Debt consolidation involves combining multiple debts into a single loan with one monthly payment, ideally at a lower interest rate. This strategy is particularly beneficial for individuals with several high-interest debts, such as credit card balances, personal loans, and other unsecured debts. By consolidating these debts into one loan, borrowers can streamline their budgeting process, reduce the risk of missed payments, and potentially lower their overall interest costs.

The primary advantage of debt consolidation lies in its simplicity. Managing a single loan payment is considerably easier than juggling multiple payments with varying due dates and interest rates. This simplification can reduce the mental and administrative burden of debt management, allowing borrowers to focus on other aspects of their financial health. Additionally, by securing a lower interest rate on the consolidated loan, borrowers can save money on interest payments over time, freeing up funds that can be redirected towards savings or other financial goals.

However, it is essential to carefully consider the terms of the new loan before proceeding with debt consolidation. Borrowers should evaluate the interest rate, repayment term, and any associated fees to ensure that the consolidation provides a genuine benefit. For instance, while the consolidated loan may offer a lower monthly payment, extending the repayment term could result in higher total interest costs over the life of the loan. Therefore, it is crucial to perform a thorough cost-benefit analysis to determine if debt consolidation is the right choice.

Refinancing

Refinancing involves replacing an existing loan with a new one, usually at a lower interest rate or with more favorable terms. This strategy can reduce monthly payments and the total amount of interest paid over the life of the loan. Refinancing is particularly advantageous for high-interest debts or when market conditions shift, offering lower interest rates than those available when the original loan was taken out.

One of the key benefits of refinancing is the potential for significant interest savings. By securing a lower interest rate, borrowers can reduce their monthly payments and overall interest costs, making it easier to manage their debt and free up cash flow for other financial priorities. Refinancing can also provide an opportunity to adjust the loan term, either shortening it to pay off the debt faster or extending it to lower monthly payments and improve short-term financial flexibility.

However, refinancing is not without its costs. Borrowers must consider various fees, such as origination fees, appraisal fees, and potential prepayment penalties on the original loan. These costs can offset the savings from a lower interest rate, so it is important to calculate the break-even point—the time it takes for the savings to outweigh the refinancing costs. A thorough analysis of these factors is essential to determine whether refinancing will provide a net financial benefit.

Evaluating the Timing and Conditions

Evaluating the timing and conditions for consolidation and refinancing is crucial for maximizing their benefits.

Several factors should be considered, including current interest rates, credit score, loan terms, and overall financial goals. A favorable interest rate environment can make both consolidation and refinancing more attractive, offering greater potential for savings. Additionally, a strong credit score can help borrowers secure better terms on the new loan, further enhancing the financial benefits.

Before proceeding with consolidation or refinancing, it is advisable to consult with a financial advisor. An expert can provide valuable insights and help determine the best course of action based on individual financial circumstances and objectives. They can also assist in navigating the complexities of loan terms and fees, ensuring that borrowers make well-informed decisions.

Not One-Size-Fits-All Solutions

Debt consolidation and refinancing are not one-size-fits-all solutions, and their effectiveness depends on the specific financial situation and goals of the borrower. For some, consolidating multiple high-interest debts into a single loan can provide much-needed simplicity and savings. For others, refinancing an existing loan at a lower interest rate can significantly reduce monthly payments and overall interest costs. Understanding the nuances of each strategy and conducting a thorough analysis of their potential benefits and costs is essential for making the right choice.

Practical Applications

In practice, debt consolidation might involve taking out a personal loan to pay off multiple credit card balances. If the personal loan has a lower interest rate than the credit cards, the borrower can save money on interest and benefit from a single, predictable monthly payment. Similarly, refinancing a mortgage to take advantage of lower interest rates can reduce monthly mortgage payments and save thousands of pounds in interest over the life of the loan.

Discipline and Commitment

Both consolidation and refinancing require a disciplined approach to ensure long-term financial benefits. Borrowers should avoid the temptation to accumulate new debt after consolidating or refinancing, as this can negate the advantages of these strategies. Maintaining a budget, focusing on debt repayment, and building an emergency fund are critical steps to achieving lasting financial stability.

Conclusion

Debt consolidation and refinancing are valuable tools for managing debt more effectively and reducing interest costs. By carefully evaluating the terms and costs associated with each strategy and consulting with financial experts, borrowers can make informed decisions that enhance their financial health and support their long-term goals. Whether seeking simplicity through consolidation or savings through refinancing, these strategies can play a pivotal role in achieving financial freedom and stability.

Chapter 3

Building Wealth Through Property

Navigating the Real Estate Market: A Path to Property Wealth

Understanding the real estate market is fundamental to building wealth through property investments. The dynamics of the market are influenced by a variety of factors, including trends, types of real estate, location, and economic and regulatory conditions. By analyzing these elements, investors can make informed decisions and strategically position themselves for long-term financial success.

Market trends are essential for real estate investors to monitor continuously. These trends include property price movements, supply and demand dynamics, and various economic indicators. Analyzing market trends involves understanding how property prices change over time and the factors driving these changes. For example, a rising market with increasing property prices might indicate strong demand and limited supply, presenting opportunities for capital gains. Conversely, a declining market may signal oversupply or reduced demand, negatively affecting property values. Economic indicators such as interest rates, inflation, and employment rates also significantly shape market trends. Low interest rates typically make borrowing more affordable, boosting demand for properties and driving up prices. Conversely, high interest rates can dampen demand as borrowing becomes more expensive. Inflation can erode purchasing power, influencing both property prices and rental yields. Employment rates affect income stability and the ability of individuals to purchase or rent properties. Staying informed about these indicators and understanding their impact on the real estate market is crucial for making well-timed investment decisions.

Understanding the different types of real estate is essential for building a diversified investment portfolio. Real estate can be broadly categorized into residential, commercial, industrial, and land, each with unique characteristics, benefits, and risks. Residential real estate includes single-family homes, apartments, and condominiums. This type of property is generally stable, with consistent demand driven by population growth and housing needs. Benefits include rental income and potential property value appreciation, though it comes with risks like tenant turnover and maintenance costs. Commercial real estate encompasses properties used for business purposes, such as office buildings, retail spaces, and hotels. Commercial properties often offer higher rental yields compared to residential properties but also come with higher risks. Economic cycles, business success, and consumer spending significantly impact demand for commercial spaces. Long-term leases in commercial properties can provide stable income, but vacancies can be prolonged and costly. Industrial real estate includes warehouses, manufacturing facilities, and distribution centers. This sector has seen growing demand driven by the rise of e-commerce and logistics. Industrial properties often offer robust rental income and lower maintenance costs. However, their value can be influenced by technological advancements and changes in industrial practices. Land investment involves purchasing undeveloped land with potential for future development. Land can appreciate significantly over time, especially if located in areas with expected growth or development. However, land investment carries risks such as zoning changes, lack of immediate income, and potential legal and environmental issues.

Location analysis is perhaps the most crucial aspect of real estate investment. The adage "location, location, location" underscores the importance of choosing properties in areas that offer the best potential for appreciation and rental income. Several factors influence property values, including proximity to amenities, quality of local schools, transport links, and future development plans. Proximity to amenities such as shopping centers, parks, and healthcare facilities enhances a property's desirability, increasing its value and rental demand. The quality of local schools is particularly significant for residential properties, as families often prioritize areas with good educational institutions. Transport links such as proximity to highways, public transportation, and airports play a vital role in determining property value. Areas with robust transport infrastructure tend to attract more buyers and tenants, driving up property values. Future development plans, such as new commercial projects or infrastructure improvements, can significantly impact property values. Thorough location research involves examining these factors, reviewing local government plans, and assessing the overall desirability of the area.

Economic and regulatory factors also profoundly influence the real estate market. Economic conditions such as interest rates, employment levels, and economic growth impact the demand and affordability of properties. Lower interest rates generally make borrowing cheaper, boosting property demand and prices. Conversely, higher interest rates can reduce affordability and dampen demand. Employment levels influence income stability, affecting individuals' ability to purchase or rent properties. Government policies and regulations, including tax policies, zoning laws, and housing regulations, shape the real estate market. Tax policies such as property taxes, capital gains taxes, and tax incentives for homebuyers can influence investment decisions. For instance, favorable tax incentives for homebuyers can stimulate demand, driving up property prices. Zoning laws regulate land use and development, affecting the types of properties that can be built in certain areas. Changes in zoning laws can either enhance or limit the potential of a property, impacting its value. Housing regulations, such as rent control policies and building codes, also affect the real estate market. Rent control policies can limit rental income potential, while stringent building codes can increase construction costs. Understanding the regulatory environment and its implications is essential for making informed investment decisions.

Navigating the real estate market requires a comprehensive understanding of market trends, types of real estate, location analysis, and economic and regulatory factors. By staying informed and strategically analyzing these elements, investors can make well-timed decisions and build a diversified property portfolio that supports long-term wealth creation. Whether investing in residential, commercial, industrial properties, or land, a deep understanding of the real estate market is key to unlocking the potential for financial growth and stability.

Stepping into Ownership: A Guide to Buying Your First Property

Purchasing your first property is a significant milestone, representing a substantial financial commitment and a crucial step towards building long-term wealth. This process requires meticulous planning, careful consideration, and informed decision-making. From financial preparation to finalizing the purchase, each stage of buying a property demands attention to detail and strategic thinking.

Financial preparation is the foundational step in buying a property. It involves saving for a down payment, improving credit scores, and understanding mortgage options to ensure affordability. Saving for a down payment is often the most challenging part for first-time buyers. Financial experts typically recommend saving at least 20% of the property's purchase price to avoid private mortgage insurance (PMI) and secure better loan terms. Setting a savings goal and creating a dedicated savings plan can help accumulate the necessary funds. Automating savings and cutting unnecessary expenses can accelerate this process.

Improving your credit score is another crucial aspect of financial preparation. A higher credit score can secure lower interest rates on mortgages, reducing the overall cost of the loan. To improve your credit score, consistently pay bills on time, reduce outstanding debts, and avoid opening new credit accounts close to the time you plan to apply for a mortgage. Regularly checking your credit report for errors and disputing any inaccuracies can also help maintain a good credit score.

Understanding mortgage options is vital for making informed financial decisions. Mortgages come in various forms, including fixed-rate, adjustable-rate, and interest-only loans. Each type has its benefits and risks. Fixed-rate mortgages offer stable monthly payments, while adjustable-rate mortgages may start with lower rates that can increase over time. Evaluating these options in the context of your financial situation and long-term plans is essential. Consulting with a mortgage advisor can provide insights into the best options available based on your credit profile and financial goals.

The property search is the next critical phase in the journey to homeownership. Finding the right property requires a combination of research, strategic planning, and professional assistance. Working with real estate agents can be highly beneficial. Agents have extensive market knowledge, access to exclusive listings, and negotiation skills that can help you find and secure the right property. They can also provide valuable insights into neighborhoods, market trends, and property values.

Attending open houses and utilizing online property listings are effective strategies for exploring available properties. Open houses allow you to see properties in person, assess their condition, and get a feel for the neighborhood. Online listings offer the convenience of browsing multiple properties at your own pace, filtering options based on your criteria, and comparing prices and features.

Creating a list of must-have features and deal-breakers is crucial for narrowing down your options. Must-have features might include the number of bedrooms and bathrooms, proximity to work or schools, and specific amenities like a garden or garage. Deal-breakers could be issues like high crime rates, poor school districts, or excessive commute times. Having a clear list helps you stay focused and make decisions aligned with your priorities.

Conducting thorough due diligence is essential to avoid potential pitfalls and ensure that the property is a sound investment. This involves home inspections, appraisals, and reviewing the property's history and title. A home inspection is a critical step that identifies any structural issues, necessary repairs, or potential problems with the property. An inspector will examine the foundation, roof, plumbing, electrical systems, and other critical components. Addressing any issues found during the inspection can prevent costly repairs down the line.

Appraisals determine the property's market value, ensuring that you are paying a fair price. Lenders typically require an appraisal to approve a mortgage. Reviewing the property's history and title is also crucial. This process involves checking for any legal issues, such as liens, disputes, or ownership claims, that could affect your ownership rights. Ensuring that the title is clear protects you from potential legal complications.

Negotiating the purchase price and terms of the sale is a critical step in securing a property at a fair value. Effective negotiation requires research, preparation, and strategic communication. Understanding the local market conditions, comparable property prices, and the seller's motivations can provide leverage in negotiations. It is essential to remain flexible and open to compromise, focusing on the overall value rather than just the price.

The closing process involves several steps, including reviewing and signing contracts, securing financing, and completing necessary paperwork. This stage can be complex and requires careful attention to detail. Reviewing contracts thoroughly ensures that all terms and conditions are clear and acceptable. Securing financing involves finalizing your mortgage, which may include additional documentation and verification by the lender. Completing the necessary paperwork involves various legal and administrative tasks, such as transferring ownership and registering the property.

Legal and financial advisors play a crucial role in ensuring a smooth transaction. A real estate lawyer can review contracts, address any legal concerns, and ensure compliance with local regulations. Financial advisors can provide guidance on managing your finances during and after the purchase, helping you stay within your budget and plan for future expenses.

Purchasing your first property is a significant financial and personal milestone that requires careful planning, informed decision-making, and professional guidance. By thoroughly preparing financially, conducting a strategic property search, performing due diligence, and navigating the negotiation and closing process effectively, you can successfully transition into homeownership. This journey, while complex, ultimately leads to securing a valuable asset that can provide long-term stability, financial growth, and personal satisfaction.

Strategic Pathways: Exploring Real Estate Investment Strategies

Investing in real estate offers a myriad of strategies, each with distinct considerations and potential returns. From long-term rental income to short-term renovation projects, real estate investments can cater to various financial goals and risk appetites. This article delves into several prominent real estate investment strategies, providing a comprehensive overview of their benefits, challenges, and potential for wealth building.

The buy and hold strategy is a classic approach in real estate investment, where investors purchase properties to rent out and retain for an extended period. This strategy focuses on generating steady rental income while benefiting from property appreciation over time. One of the primary advantages of buy and hold is the consistent cash flow from rental payments. This income can provide financial stability and support other investment endeavors. Additionally, property values tend to appreciate over the long term, offering the potential for significant capital gains when the property is eventually sold. However, the buy and hold strategy also comes with responsibilities and challenges. Effective property management is crucial to maintaining the property's value and ensuring a steady income stream. This includes tasks such as tenant screening, lease management, maintenance, and addressing tenant issues. Investors must be prepared for periods of vacancy and potential repairs, which can impact cash flow. Despite these challenges, the buy and hold strategy remains a popular choice for those seeking long-term wealth accumulation and passive income.

Flipping properties is another popular real estate investment strategy that involves purchasing properties, renovating them, and selling them for a profit. This approach can yield substantial returns in a relatively short period, but it requires a keen eye for property selection and effective project management. The key to successful flipping lies in choosing properties with strong potential for improvement and resale value. Investors must conduct thorough market research to identify undervalued properties in desirable locations. Managing renovation costs is critical to maximizing profits. Investors need to budget accurately, hire reliable contractors, and oversee the renovation process to ensure quality and timeliness. Market timing also plays a vital role in flipping properties. Selling during a seller's market, where demand outstrips supply, can lead to higher sale prices and quicker transactions. However, flipping properties carries inherent risks, such as fluctuating market conditions, unforeseen renovation expenses, and the possibility of prolonged holding periods if the property does not sell quickly. Investors must be prepared for these uncertainties and have contingency plans in place.

Real Estate Investment Trusts (REITs) offer an alternative way to invest in real estate without directly owning property.

REITs are companies that own, operate, or finance income-producing real estate across various sectors. They allow individual investors to purchase shares and gain exposure to real estate assets, benefiting from the income generated by these properties. REITs are typically traded on major stock exchanges, providing liquidity and ease of entry and exit compared to direct property ownership. There are different types of REITs, including equity REITs, which own and manage real estate properties, and mortgage REITs, which provide financing for income-producing real estate by purchasing or originating mortgages and mortgage-backed securities. The benefits of investing in REITs include diversification, professional management, and attractive dividend yields. REITs must distribute at least 90% of their taxable income to shareholders, resulting in regular income streams. Evaluating REITs involves analyzing factors such as the quality and performance of the underlying properties, the REIT's management team, and its financial health. Including REITs in an investment portfolio can provide a balanced exposure to real estate with reduced risks compared to direct ownership.

Commercial real estate presents another compelling investment opportunity, encompassing properties such as office buildings, retail spaces, and industrial facilities. Investing in commercial real estate offers the potential for higher rental yields compared to residential properties, as businesses often pay a premium for prime locations and amenities. Commercial properties also tend to have longer lease terms, providing more stable and predictable income streams. However, commercial real estate investment requires a different set of considerations and expertise. Lease terms in commercial real estate are more complex and varied than residential leases, often involving triple net leases where tenants are responsible for property taxes, insurance, and maintenance. This can reduce the landlord's operational burdens but requires careful lease structuring and tenant management. The market dynamics of commercial real estate are closely tied to economic cycles, consumer behavior, and business trends. For example, the rise of e-commerce has increased demand for industrial properties, while traditional retail spaces have faced challenges. Successful commercial real estate investment involves thorough due diligence, including assessing the location, quality of the property, tenant mix, and lease terms. Investors must also stay informed about market trends and economic indicators that impact commercial real estate. Engaging with professional property managers and commercial real estate brokers can provide valuable insights and support in navigating this complex market.

Each real estate investment strategy offers unique benefits and challenges, catering to different investment objectives and risk tolerances. The buy and hold strategy provides steady rental income and long-term appreciation, making it suitable for those seeking passive income and long-term wealth building. Flipping properties offers the potential for high short-term returns but requires active management and market acumen. REITs provide a way to invest in real estate without direct ownership, offering liquidity, diversification, and regular income. Commercial real estate can yield higher returns and longer leases but demands specialized knowledge and careful market analysis. Understanding these strategies and their implications is crucial for making informed investment decisions. By aligning investment choices with financial goals, risk tolerance, and market conditions, investors can build a diversified and resilient real estate portfolio. Whether aiming for steady income, short-term gains, or diversified exposure, real estate offers a rich array of opportunities for building wealth and achieving financial security.

Enhancing Wealth: Strategies for Maximising Property Value

Maximising the value of your property is essential for building wealth through real estate. By strategically enhancing your property, managing it effectively, and leveraging financial tools, you can significantly increase its market value and rental income potential. This involves renovations, property management, rental income optimisation, marketing, and understanding tax benefits.

Strategic renovations and upgrades are powerful tools for increasing property value. Investing in improvements that offer the best return on investment (ROI) can enhance the property's appeal and functionality, making it more attractive to potential buyers or tenants. One of the most effective areas to focus on is the kitchen. A modern, well-equipped kitchen can significantly boost property value, as it is often considered the heart of the home. Upgrades such as new countertops, energy-efficient appliances, and updated cabinetry can yield substantial returns. Similarly, bathroom remodels are another high-ROI improvement. Replacing outdated fixtures, adding new tiling, and installing efficient water-saving devices can enhance the appeal and functionality of bathrooms. Landscaping is also a crucial factor in increasing property value. A well-maintained garden with attractive plants, trees, and outdoor living spaces can create a positive first impression and increase the property's curb appeal. Energy-efficient installations, such as solar panels, double-glazed windows, and improved insulation, can reduce utility costs and appeal to environmentally conscious buyers or tenants, further boosting property value.

Effective property management plays a vital role in maintaining and increasing property value. Proper management ensures that the property remains in good condition, tenants are satisfied, and rental income is maximised. One of the key aspects of property management is tenant screening. Thorough screening processes help select reliable tenants who are more likely to pay rent on time and take care of the property. Establishing clear and fair lease agreements is also crucial. Well-drafted leases protect both the landlord and tenant, clearly outlining responsibilities, terms, and conditions. Regular maintenance and prompt repairs are essential for preserving property value. Routine inspections and maintenance schedules can prevent minor issues from becoming costly repairs. Addressing problems promptly not only maintains the property's condition but also keeps tenants satisfied and reduces turnover rates. Hiring a professional property management company can be highly beneficial. Experienced property managers handle day-to-day operations, tenant interactions, maintenance, and legal matters, ensuring that the property is managed efficiently and effectively.

Increasing rental income is another strategy to maximise property value. By implementing various enhancements and management techniques, landlords can attract higher rents and improve their property's profitability. Adding amenities such as in-unit laundry, high-speed internet, or upgraded kitchen appliances can justify higher rental rates. Allowing pets can also be a lucrative decision, as many tenants are willing to pay extra for pet-friendly accommodations. However, it's important to establish clear pet policies to mitigate potential issues. Implementing lease renewals with rent increases is a strategic way to boost rental income without the need for frequent tenant turnover. Understanding the rental market is crucial for setting competitive yet profitable rental rates.

Conducting market research to compare similar properties in the area can help determine appropriate rental pricing. Offering short-term incentives, such as a one-month free rent for signing a longer lease, can also attract tenants while securing longer occupancy periods.

Marketing and curb appeal play a significant role in attracting quality tenants or buyers and maximising property value. The way a property is presented can greatly influence its perceived value. Staging a property effectively showcases its potential, making it easier for prospective tenants or buyers to envision themselves living there. Professional photography captures the property's best features, making it stand out in online listings. High-quality images and virtual tours can attract more interest and lead to quicker, higher offers. Curb appeal is equally important. The exterior of the property is the first thing people see, and a positive first impression can significantly impact their perception of the property's value. Simple improvements like fresh paint, clean windows, and well-maintained landscaping can enhance curb appeal. Ensuring that pathways are clear, the lawn is mowed, and the entrance is inviting creates a welcoming atmosphere that appeals to potential tenants or buyers.

Leveraging tax benefits is another effective way to maximise property value. Tax deductions for mortgage interest, property taxes, and depreciation can significantly reduce the overall cost of owning and maintaining a property. Mortgage interest deductions allow property owners to deduct the interest paid on their mortgage from their taxable income, reducing their tax liability. Property tax deductions enable owners to deduct the amount paid in property taxes, further lowering their taxable income. Depreciation is a powerful tax benefit that allows property owners to deduct the cost of the property over its useful life. This deduction can offset rental income, reducing the amount of taxable income and potentially resulting in significant tax savings. Keeping accurate records of all expenses related to the property is essential for claiming these deductions. Working with a tax professional ensures compliance with tax laws and maximises the benefits of available deductions.

Maximising property value requires a multifaceted approach that includes strategic renovations, effective property management, rental income optimisation, impactful marketing, and leveraging tax benefits. By implementing these strategies, property owners can enhance their property's appeal, increase profitability, and build long-term wealth through real estate. Each strategy contributes to the overall value of the property, ensuring that it remains a valuable asset in the owner's investment portfolio. Through careful planning and execution, maximising property value becomes a tangible goal, leading to sustained financial growth and stability.

Chapter 4

Investing for Wealth

Introduction

Investing for wealth is a sophisticated endeavor that goes beyond mere financial transactions; it is an art that requires strategic planning, informed decision-making, and a thorough understanding of market dynamics. In an increasingly complex financial landscape, mastering the principles of investment is essential for anyone seeking to build and preserve wealth over the long term. This chapter delves into the intricacies of investing, offering a comprehensive guide to developing a robust investment strategy that aligns with your financial goals and risk tolerance.

At its core, investing is about putting your money to work to generate returns over time. It is a disciplined approach to building wealth that involves allocating capital to various financial instruments, such as stocks, bonds, real estate, and other assets, with the expectation of achieving positive returns. The fundamental principle of investing is the trade-off between risk and return. Higher returns are typically associated with higher risks, while lower-risk investments generally offer more modest returns. Understanding this relationship is crucial for making informed investment decisions.

One of the key aspects of investing for wealth is recognizing the power of compounding. Compounding occurs when the returns on an investment are reinvested, generating additional returns over time. This process can lead to exponential growth of your investment portfolio, significantly enhancing wealth accumulation. The earlier you start investing, the more time your investments have to compound, making time one of the most valuable assets in the investment process.

Creating an investment portfolio that balances risk and return is a critical step in wealth building. This involves diversifying your investments across different asset classes to mitigate risk and maximize potential returns. Diversification reduces the impact of poor performance in any single investment, thereby enhancing the stability of your overall portfolio. A well-diversified portfolio typically includes a mix of equities, fixed income, real estate, and other assets, each contributing to the overall growth and resilience of your investments.

Long-term investment strategies are essential for sustained wealth creation. Unlike short-term trading, which seeks to capitalize on market fluctuations, long-term investing focuses on holding investments over extended periods, allowing them to grow and compound. This approach not only reduces transaction costs but also minimizes the impact of market volatility, which can be detrimental to short-term gains. By adopting a long-term perspective, investors can better withstand market downturns and benefit from the overall upward trajectory of financial markets.

Monitoring and adjusting your investment portfolio is an ongoing process that ensures your investments remain aligned with your financial goals and market conditions. Regularly reviewing your portfolio allows you to assess its performance, identify any deviations from your investment strategy, and make necessary adjustments. This may involve rebalancing your portfolio to maintain your desired asset allocation, adding new investments, or divesting underperforming assets. Staying informed about economic and market developments is crucial for making timely and informed adjustments to your investment strategy.

Investing for wealth also involves understanding the various types of investments and how they fit into your overall financial plan. Equities, for instance, represent ownership in a company and offer the potential for high returns through capital appreciation and dividends. However, they also come with higher risk due to market volatility. Bonds, on the other hand, are fixed-income securities that provide regular interest payments and are generally considered lower risk compared to equities. Real estate investments offer the benefits of rental income and property appreciation, while alternative investments such as commodities and private equity can provide diversification and unique return opportunities.

The role of tax planning in investing for wealth cannot be overstated. Tax-efficient investing involves strategies that minimize tax liabilities and maximize after-tax returns. This includes taking advantage of tax-advantaged accounts such as Individual Savings Accounts (ISAs) and pensions, understanding the tax implications of different investments, and utilizing tax loss harvesting to offset gains. Working with a tax professional can help you navigate the complexities of tax regulations and optimize your investment strategy.

One of the most challenging aspects of investing is managing emotions. Market fluctuations can evoke fear and greed, leading to impulsive decisions that can undermine long-term investment success. Developing a disciplined approach to investing, guided by a well-thought-out plan and clear financial goals, is essential for maintaining focus and avoiding emotional pitfalls. Sticking to your investment strategy, even during periods of market turbulence, can significantly enhance your chances of achieving your financial objectives.

Education and continuous learning are vital components of successful investing. The financial markets are dynamic, influenced by a myriad of factors including economic indicators, geopolitical events, and technological advancements. Staying informed about market trends, investment strategies, and financial news helps you make informed decisions and adapt to changing conditions. There are numerous resources available for investors, including books, online courses, financial advisors, and investment seminars. Engaging with these resources can deepen your understanding of investing and enhance your ability to build and preserve wealth.

In essence, investing for wealth is a multifaceted endeavor that requires a blend of knowledge, discipline, and strategic planning. By understanding the basics of investing, creating a diversified portfolio, adopting long-term strategies, and continuously monitoring and adjusting your investments, you can build a solid foundation for financial success. The journey of investing is not without its challenges, but with a thoughtful approach and a commitment to your financial goals, you can navigate the complexities of the financial markets and achieve sustained wealth over time.

Foundations of Prosperity: The Basics of Investing

Understanding the fundamentals of investing is essential for building wealth and achieving financial goals. Investing is not merely about allocating money into different assets; it is a disciplined approach that involves strategic planning, risk management, and a deep understanding of market dynamics. This article delves into the core principles of investing, various types of investments, investment accounts, and the critical aspects of fees and taxes.

The core principles of investing are the bedrock upon which successful investment strategies are built. One of the most fundamental principles is the relationship between risk and return. Generally, investments with higher potential returns come with higher levels of risk. Understanding this trade-off is crucial for making informed investment decisions. Investors need to assess their risk tolerance, which is their ability and willingness to endure market volatility and potential losses in pursuit of higher returns. This assessment helps in selecting investments that align with one's financial goals and comfort level with risk.

Diversification is another key principle of investing. This strategy involves spreading investments across various asset classes and sectors to reduce exposure to any single investment's risks. Diversification can mitigate the impact of poor performance in one investment by balancing it with better performance in others. For instance, a diversified portfolio might include stocks, bonds, real estate, and commodities, each contributing to the overall stability and growth of the portfolio. The objective is to optimise the balance between risk and return, enhancing the potential for long-term wealth creation.

The power of compounding is a powerful principle that significantly contributes to wealth accumulation over time. Compounding occurs when the returns on an investment generate additional returns. For example, interest earned on a savings account or dividends received from stocks can be reinvested, leading to exponential growth of the initial investment. The earlier one starts investing, the more time there is for compounding to work its magic, making time a crucial factor in investment success.

There are various types of investments, each with its own characteristics, benefits, and risks. Stocks represent ownership in a company and offer the potential for high returns through capital appreciation and dividends. However, stocks are also subject to market volatility, and their prices can fluctuate significantly. Bonds, on the other hand, are fixed-income securities that provide regular interest payments and are generally considered lower risk compared to stocks. They are typically used to provide stability and income within a portfolio. Mutual funds and exchange-traded funds (ETFs) are pooled investment vehicles that offer diversification by investing in a broad range of assets. Mutual funds are actively managed, meaning fund managers make decisions about which securities to buy and sell. ETFs, meanwhile, are typically passively managed and aim to replicate the performance of a specific index. Both mutual funds and ETFs provide investors with an easy way to diversify their investments without needing to select individual securities. Real estate investments involve purchasing properties to generate rental income or capital appreciation. Real estate can provide a steady income stream and has the potential for long-term appreciation. However, it also requires significant capital and active management. Commodities, such as gold, oil, and agricultural products, are another investment option. They can serve as a hedge against inflation and diversify a portfolio but are often subject to price volatility.

Investment accounts are the vehicles through which individuals invest in various assets. Individual brokerage accounts offer flexibility and control, allowing investors to buy and sell a wide range of securities. However, these accounts are subject to capital gains taxes on any profits realised from investments. Retirement accounts, such as Individual Retirement Accounts (IRAs) and 401(k)s, provide tax advantages that can enhance long-term savings. Traditional IRAs and 401(k)s offer tax-deferred growth, meaning that investments grow tax-free until withdrawals are made during retirement. Roth IRAs, on the other hand, allow for tax-free withdrawals in retirement, as contributions are made with after-tax dollars. Health Savings Accounts (HSAs) are another type of tax-advantaged account that offers triple tax benefits: contributions are tax-deductible, investments grow tax-free, and withdrawals for qualified medical expenses are tax-free.

Understanding the fees and taxes associated with investing is critical for maximising returns. Fees can significantly erode investment returns over time. Common fees include management fees, which are charged by fund managers for managing mutual funds or ETFs, and trading commissions, which are fees paid to brokers for executing buy or sell orders. Expense ratios, which represent the annual cost of managing a fund as a percentage of the fund's assets, are also an important consideration when selecting investments. Taxes can also have a substantial impact on investment returns. Capital gains taxes are levied on the profits realised from selling investments. Short-term capital gains, from investments held for less than a year, are taxed at ordinary income tax rates, while long-term capital gains, from investments held for more than a year, are taxed at lower rates. Dividend income is also subject to taxes, although qualified dividends are taxed at a lower rate than ordinary income. Investors can employ various strategies to minimise tax liabilities. Tax-loss harvesting involves selling investments that have declined in value to offset gains from other investments, thereby reducing overall capital gains taxes. Contributing to tax-advantaged accounts, such as IRAs and 401(k)s, can also provide tax benefits that enhance long-term savings. Engaging with a financial advisor or tax professional can help investors navigate the complexities of fees and taxes, ensuring that their investment strategies are optimised for maximum returns.

Understanding the basics of investing is essential for building wealth and achieving financial goals. By adhering to core investment principles, diversifying investments, utilising appropriate investment accounts, and managing fees and taxes, investors can develop a robust strategy that supports long-term financial success. Investing is a journey that requires knowledge, discipline, and a willingness to adapt to changing market conditions. With a solid foundation in the fundamentals of investing, individuals can confidently navigate the financial markets and work towards their wealth-building objectives.

Crafting a Robust Investment Portfolio: Strategies for Success

It is important to diversify your investments so as to reduce risk and maximize return. A well thought out portfolio consists of different kinds of investments that are consistent with one's financial goals and risk tolerance thereby laying a firm ground for accumulation of wealth over a long period of time. This write-up gives an insight into what makes up an investment portfolio creation process; starting from setting investment objectives to choosing specific securities hence providing extensive knowledge for any investor who would wish to have a strong investment base.

The initial stage of forming an investment portfolio is by defining what you want to achieve from the investment. These should be clear and precise so as not to deviate in the strategy. The goals could range widely such as saving for retirement, college fee funding, buying a house or even becoming financially independent. These can only be realized after assessing oneself financially i.e. the needs and dreams they have. For example if someone's main aim is to save money for use during their old age then it means that they must first find out how much will be required annually in order live comfortably without any financial hitches thus taking into account life expectancy at that particular period when this person would have retired also keeping inflation into consideration among other things like at what age do we expect most people start retiring etc. It is important that we only invest in line with our stated objectives failure of which may lead us to meeting something else with our finances which was not intended initially by us. To demonstrate with another instance; where one has got short term goals say building a house through savings realized from monthly income then certainly such an individual should adopt quite safe approaches towards handling their money since they might need it any time soon before completion date gets nearer and so on.

One's portfolio has to reflect their aims at all times thus regular reviews as well as updates become necessary for this case. Situations change and therefore adjustments must be made where necessary lest the current status quo becomes irrelevant or incapable of yielding results. In pursuit of different financial goals, one should be ready and willing to use corresponding investment strategies alongside them each time the need arises. For instance those planning on retiring are advised to invest more in shares due higher returns expected over long term unlike people who are saving towards buying homes; these group needs lower risk investments that guarantees preservation of capital as much as possible while giving modest profits in short run also known as bonds among others Lastly let us never forget this fact; what may seem appropriate today could easily become obsolete tomorrow thus rendering us bankrupt if we don't keep pace with these changes in various sectors of economy where our interests lie.

Your investment strategy needs to take into account your risk tolerance and time horizon. Risk tolerance indicates a person's ability to endure fluctuations in investment value and is determined by emotional and financial considerations. Some people are more inclined towards stable low-risk investments while others are prepared to take higher risks for higher returns. The amount of time that you expect to keep an investment before needing funds also affects your risk tolerance. Generally speaking, longer periods allow for greater levels because there is more opportunity to recover from any market setbacks. The relationship between risk and potential returns is one of the fundamental concepts of investment. Normally speaking, there are higher chances of getting larger returns when there is more risk involved and vice versa. These must be harmonized in a single portfolio so that risk is managed while investment objectives are met. It is difficult if not impossible to overemphasize the importance of diversification. Diversifying across asset classes helps balance reward against jeopardy which can enhance long-term growth potential while alleviating market twists impact. Asset allocation refers to dividing investments among different types of securities with varied levels of risk and return potential so as to strike this balance.

Asset classes are the categories of investments into which you can place your money; they include stocks, bonds, real estate, and cash equivalents. Equities generally produce higher returns but also come with greater price fluctuations. Fixed income securities like bonds offer stable income flow because interest rates do not change very often however this means that their prices are likely to change when rates go up or down which leads them having lower risks compared to shares whose dividends depend on company performance thus making it risky especially during economic downturns where most companies make losses hence their value depreciates rapidly inline with market conditions if not worse off than before hence they become highly volatile hence would require active management strategies like buying when low selling high among others Real estate provides an opportunity for capital growth through appreciation over time plus earning rental income but it needs constant attention due maintenance issues among other things Cash equivalents are financial instruments that can be easily converted into cash such as money market funds certificate deposits treasury bills etc these types offer quick accessibility along with safety at the expense of lower returns Also knowning where to invest your finances in can make all the difference for example knowing when and where to invest in these funds could result in a significant increase compared if one puts his/her money elsewhere

To choose particular investments in each group of assets, careful study and analysis must be conducted. For example, equities can be selected using criteria like company fundamentals; market trends; and economic situations among others. Financial statements need to be scrutinized when evaluating performance whereby one has to understand different business models while at the same time critically examining competitive advantages associated with them all. Bonds on their part demand consideration such as credit worthinesses as well as environments for interest rates including durations.

Real estate necessitates market research concerning properties available for sale or rent within specific locations; potential incomes from rentals vis a vis costs involved in managing such facilities among other things need be looked into thoroughly before any decision is arrived at. The importance of conducting research before making investments cannot be overstated. To begin with, company fundamentals reveal much about the financial strength and future prospects of a firm. Such basics may consist of earnings growth rates; profitability margins achieved over certain periods coupled with debt levels sustained by an organization over time. In addition, trends within sectors should not escape our attention since they give an insight into how the wider economy is faring on the whole. Moreover, factors like interest rates; inflation rates and geopolitical events have direct effect on investment climate thereby influencing performance of various assets classes respectively. As a matter of fact, one should take into account costs associated with investing.

It is necessary to minimize expenses as much as possible to enhance the net income in the long run. Fees charged for managing investments can eat into returns significantly if not properly monitored hence the need for comparison among different alternatives available based on expense ratios; trading commissions charged per transaction made relative to volume handled by such brokerages over specified period(s). Furthermore, creating an investment portfolio does not stop once it has been established but rather becomes a continuous process that calls for regular reviews and adjustments. This is because the value of securities changes overtime depending on market conditions thus affecting asset allocation which may require rebalancing so as to maintain desired mix within given limits . For instance , engaging services offered by financial advisors would serve good purpose towards this end .A financial advisor plays a crucial role in helping individuals come up with suitable plans depending on their particular circumstances .In order to achieve maximum benefits from investments people should establish clear objectives backed by realistic expectations while at same time taking into consideration personal risk tolerance levels .This can only be achieved effectively if one seeks professional advice from qualified experts who have vast experience knowledge base about various types capital markets instruments available globally today . By so doing , they will also get access new insights markets trends recommend specific investment opportunities carrying out regular monitoring such recommendations facilitate achievement desirable outcomes within predetermined time frames . Therefore , anyone serious about growing wealth needs realize importance having sound strategies all times .

To create an investment portfolio is a complex process. This involves setting goals, evaluating how much risk can be taken, distributing resources and choosing where to invest. If people stick to these rules and handle the matter orderly, they may accumulate long-standing monetary assets that can withstand different economic times. When done well thought out regularly reviewed an investment portfolio becomes a powerful instrument for achieving financial success and security.

Strategies for Enduring Wealth: Long-Term Investment Approaches

To amass and maintain prosperity, it is necessary to follow good long-term investment strategies. To establish financial goals, these strategies rely on waiting, control, and tactical planning. This commentary examines the main long-term investment policies, such as buy and hold, dollar-cost averaging, growth versus value investing, and why it is important to rebalance a portfolio regularly as they can help in continuous wealth creation.

Long term investment is based on the buy-and-hold strategy. Under this tactic, an investor buys securities with no plan of selling them in the near future regardless of what happens in the market. The theory behind this strategy is that over a long period most markets have shown an upward trend despite short-term price volatility. By enduring through periods when prices are rising or falling dramatically investors may take advantage of general market growth. Lowering transaction costs is one of the main advantages associated with using buy-and-hold method. The more one trades; the higher their expenditure becomes due to taxes as well as commissions incurred from frequent transactions thereby reducing their earnings on those investments overall. Also, this technique utilizes compound interest which refers to reinvesting profits realized from an asset back into itself so that they can earn even more thus causing exponential growth over time . Consequently, if held for many years compounding stands out as a powerful tool for amassing wealth.

One more useful long-term investment strategy is dollar-cost averaging. It means that an investor should spend a fixed amount of money at a certain period of time no matter what is happening in the market. When the prices are low, the fixed amount buys more shares; when high, it buys fewer shares. This way, the cost per share is averaged over time. Such an approach helps to reduce the impact of market volatility and avoid badly timed investment decisions. Following dollar-cost averaging develops a habit of disciplined investment; thus making regular saving and investment possible for people who might not have skills or confidence necessary for timing the market . In the end, it leads to lower average costs for investments made over the years which in turn improves total returns and maintains steady growth over time.

"Growth" and "value" are two different methods of choosing stocks; each having its own advantages and disadvantages. The first type concentrates on those companies that are expected to have a higher-than-average growth rate vis-à-vis others. Normally, such companies plough back their profits into business expansion, new product development or entry into new markets. Growth stocks offer potential for high returns but at the same time subject investors to increased volatility and risk. Investors must be prepared for huge price swings and failure by such firms to realize anticipated growth. On the other hand, value investing entails identifying undervalued shares capable of appreciation. This means looking for companies whose stocks may not be reflecting their true worth due to temporary setbacks or market overreactions. The main idea behind this strategy is buying these securities cheaper with a view of benefiting from future price adjustments upwards. Generally considered less risky than growth investing because it centers around businesses with strong balance sheets and consistent earnings, value investment could be time-consuming as the market may take long before it corrects undervaluation.

Rebalancing is an important long-term investment strategy that helps to keep the portfolio in line with the investor's objectives and risk tolerance. As time passes, movements of the markets might cause different assets in a portfolio to have different values. For example, if stocks perform very well they could take a larger percentage of the portfolio than was originally planned thereby increasing overall risk level. This process includes periodically readjusting one's holdings so as restore them back their initial levels which is also known as rebalancing. In essence this means selling off those investments with good performance and buying those which have underperformed thereby 'selling high buying low'. By doing so it becomes possible not only manages risks across different types of securities within an account but also ensures that it captures other benefits associated with such actions.

These types of strategies require an understanding individual needs such as financial goals, risk tolerance levels or even investment horizons among others. There are numerous strategies that can be used for long term investments. One such strategy is the 'buy and hold' approach that is suitable for individuals who have patience coupled with stable emotions towards various market cycles within the economy. This method aims at reducing transaction costs while at the same time letting returns compound over time hence it should only be applied by people looking forward to retiring many years from now Dollar cost averaging offers investors a chance to buy more shares when prices are low and fewer when they are high thus minimizing potential losses due sudden changes in value associated with specific investments Which types of stocks should I invest in Growth vs value Investing: Growth investing focuses on companies expected to grow earnings at above-average rates compared to other firms same size within their industry Value investing concentrates more towards identifying undervalued securities either relative historical benchmarks like P/E ratio book value per share etc allowing investors take advantage temporary mispricing's while waiting until market fully recognizes true worth of these undervalued assets The information provided above is meant to serve as a general knowledge base for investors and should not be considered personal financial advice

To prevent deviating from the objectives and risk tolerance of the investor the portfolio should be realigned through rebalancing which ensures effective risk management by asset classes still being within their stipulated proportions every now and then. When investors periodically review their portfolios while making necessary adjustments they are able to keep track with their long-term financial plans.

Generally speaking, building and protecting wealth requires a holistic approach provided by such long-term investment strategies as dollar-cost averaging, buying and holding growth stocks versus value stocks among others like this. These methods based on patience, discipline combined with strategic placements serve well during different market cycles thus helping in realizing maximum returns over time through reduction or neutralization of effects caused by volatility. A good understanding of these approaches coupled with their application can result into strong investment portfolios that foster continuous income generation as well as securing one's future financially.

On Guard for Success: Keeping Your Portfolio in Tune

One of the most important things you can do to get where you want to be financially is often reviewing and adjusting your investment portfolio since market dynamics, personal situations as well as economic environments change. With this in mind, a proactive approach towards managing your investments becomes necessary. This article looks into evaluating performance, recognizing shifts in goals and circumstances, comprehending economic conditions' impact on markets or industries among others then making appropriate changes that will keep an individual's long-term objectives aligned with their investment portfolio.

Analyzing how well an investment portfolio has done is a key part of managing investments effectively. This includes such activities as calculating returns; comparing them with relevant benchmarks and evaluating risk-adjusted performance. Calculating returns involves finding out how much money the total investment has made or lost during a certain time period which includes capital gains from selling assets for more than they were bought at originally plus any income received like dividends or interest on bonds. Raw return figures only give a brief idea about performance therefore these should also be looked at in relation to some standard measure known as benchmark(s). In this case market indices can act as benchmarks against which one may compare their own performance while attempting to achieve similar results within given risk parameters.

Another important thing that should be considered when evaluating performance is the level of risks taken into account so far if any returns were actually realized. One good example would be Sharpe ratio which measures excess return per unit deviation from mean return; thus indicating whether high profits were earned through taking huge risks or not. It should be noted that different investments have different level of risks thus there is no one-size-fits-all approach in this regard. Regular review of performance becomes necessary so as to ensure that investments are on track towards meeting their intended purposes vis-à-vis financial planning objectives broadly defined. If any underperforming assets/strategies are identified during such analyses then appropriate actions must immediately follow suit which may range from reallocation all way up adjustments either through selling some securities while buying others alternatively changing entire funds involved altogether.

It is essential to review your investment strategy regularly to take into consideration changes in your personal circumstances and goals. Changes in income, family situation, or major financial milestones significantly affect investment needs and risk tolerance. For example, if someone earns much more than before, they may be able to save greater amounts for investments; alternatively if their income falls short it might demand for more conservative approach. Also, changes in family set-ups such as getting married/divorced/ having children could alter financial priorities thereby calling for different types of assets allocations or investment strategies.

Decisions regarding investments can be greatly influenced by key moments in life such as retirement and inheritance reception. Normally people stop working when they reach old age which means they will not have any more salaries coming in every month; this therefore requires one to think about how best generate income from what had been saved up until then while still keeping some aside for emergencies etcetera. The focus also shifts towards keeping rather than making money during this period hence lower risk income producing ventures should take priority over high return but risky ones. On the other hand getting left with money or property through death of family members might present chances for improving returns through wider spread but care must be taken so that new assets are well amalgamated into existing ones.

It is impossible to overstate the importance of being aware about economic conditions when managing portfolios effectively. Things such as interest rates, inflation rates and political instability among others have great impact on how well different types of investments perform over time; therefore any serious investor must keep an eye on them if they want their wealth grow steadily. Interest being cost money borrowed against it them (bonds) while at same time increases prices everything else also because now there are more dollars chasing fewer goods this leads us into another thing called "purchasing power" basically refers what can be bought with certain amount funds usually expressed terms percentage change value currency some index reflecting general level prices within economy geopolitical matters like war tariffs etcetera create conditions under which stock markets become turbulent affecting both local foreign securities negatively.

The following are crucial for content writing:

Perplexity: It is the measure of how strange a text is to large language models like ChatGPT.

Burstiness: A unique score used by GPTZero in 2022 that quantifies variance in writing – humans usually vary their writing patterns over time.

Readability: High readability scores are achieved through the use of short words with low syllable count in sentences.

Simplicity: This measures what percentage of words come from the top 100 most common English language terms.

Average Sentence Length: It is a unique score for determining variance in writing, where humans generally vary writing patterns.

Percent SAT: This measures what percentage of words are from SAT, which refers to a labyrinthine vocabulary list recognized for its use in a standardized college admissions exam (Scholastic Assessment Test)

Portfolio management requires a long-term perspective. Even though it 's unsettling to witness constant shifts in the short-term market, one can be discouraged from acting on momentary volatilities by keeping their focus on ultimate objectives. The strategy should be based on regular monitoring and adjustment of the portfolio. This means that any changes made will not be sudden but well thought out since they are in line with the laid-down procedures for making decisions concerning investments.

Performance assessment should take place periodically. Reviews could be done after every three months (quarterly), six months (semi-annually), or one year (annually). During such times, investors get an opportunity to measure how well or bad different assets have done against each other in terms of attaining their desired results financially speaking alongside any alterations that may have occurred either within them or around them vis-à-vis this goal. Essentially what needs checking at these points would be; has there been a change in asset allocation? Has any security performed better than others? Are we still on track towards meeting our long-term financial objectives?

In conclusion, it is crucial for individuals to review their investment portfolio on a regular basis so as not lose sight of where they want to be financially. To keep in line with this, they should also respond appropriately when things change regarding their personal circumstances or even global economic conditions. In other words, by being aware of what's happening out there investors will know when and how best adjust various elements within this bundle of securities that has been put together over time if any meaningful success is to be achieved in future times.

Chapter 5

Securing Tomorrow: Planning for Retirement

Introduction

According to the experts, personal finance can never be whole without retirement planning. It involves creating different methods of guaranteeing financial security and a good quality life in the future years after one has stopped working. People should plan for their retirement in a uniform manner at all times during employment years due to its importance. It goes beyond saving money each month but taking into account several things such as how long someone expects to live since this will determine whether they might need more than what is being saved now because inflation rates never remain constant over any given period. Additionally many will go through various health challenges thus incur high medical expenses which also need consideration while still young enough so as not face hardships later when these costs become inevitable or perhaps desired standards change as time goes by though this may happen rarely among other factors.

The gravity of retirement planning is that it brings about financial security as well as peace of mind. This is highlighted by the fact that traditional pension schemes have become less common in today's world while government support alone cannot sustain an individual throughout their elderly years hence the need for personal savings towards retirement. To add on this good planning ensures one does not exhaust all their savings before they die especially now when people are living longer than ever before following successful health interventions which have been made possible due to improved medical care systems globally thereby raising life expectancy rates significantly worldwide over recent decades resulting into longer post-working periods requiring higher financial support levels if standard living are maintainable.

Another basic rule of retirement planning entails understanding different types of retirement accounts available plus their respective advantages. According to any well-versed person who knows much about retiring, he or she should be familiar with such terms as Individual Retirement Accounts (IRAs) or even 401(k)s since these two usually act like foundation stones upon which most people's retirement strategies lie. Every account has its own benefits but what makes them stand out from each other are the tax advantages that come along with it so you need to understand this well lest mistakes occur later when trying to access your money particularly after attaining the age of 59½ years unless certain conditions have been met before then if not otherwise stated expressly by law because failure may attract heavy penalties upon withdrawal among other related issues for which legal advice would help.

The process of saving for retirement has never been easier, but there are many options to consider depending on your situation. There are a few different types of retirement accounts you can use depending on if you work for yourself or someone else. For example, if you work for an employer that offers a 401(k), then this might be the best option because they will often match some percentage with their own money which is like getting free cash. Or if instead, you are self-employed and do not have any employees (besides spouse), then setting up either a traditional IRA or a SEP-IRA could make sense since these allow much larger annual contributions than most other types of accounts do while still providing valuable tax deductions now and in the future when withdrawing during retirement years.

For instance, if you're self-employed, you could contribute up to $58,000 in 2021 across all your IRA and 401(k) accounts, assuming you're under 50 years old. This can help reduce your taxable income now while setting aside money for the future. The key is to start as soon as possible so that compound interest has time to work its magic on those savings! Plus there are some great tax benefits available if done correctly such as deducting contributions from current-year taxes owed or possibly even getting a credit against them instead.

In conclusion, retirement planning is not something that can be done overnight. It takes time and careful consideration to ensure you're making the right decisions for your future. By understanding the different types of accounts available, how they work, and their respective benefits, you'll be better equipped to save more effectively in preparation for this exciting new chapter in life!

Creating an effective savings plan for retirement requires establishing specific achievable objectives rooted in an individual's future financial requirements. The first step in this process is to determine how much money will be needed annually during retirement years to support oneself comfortably. Considerations include housing costs as well as everyday living expenses like food and clothing among others; healthcare such as insurance premiums or long-term care coverage may also need consideration along with recreational activities that bring joy into one's life. Furthermore, potential revenue streams like social security benefits (if any), pension payouts from former employers etc., part-time work earnings should all be taken into account for proper planning towards saving up for retirement. Forecasting what your future income will look alike vis-a-vis outlays helps lay down the most appropriate strategy regarding which investment vehicles require what amounts should they produce quarterly before-tax return annually Post Tax Return Net Worth Value Final Maturity Amount rate of interest duration years months fortnightly weekly daily hourly be put in saving

Another key element of an efficient savings plan for retirement is discipline when it comes to saving and investing. The significance of compounding interest cannot be overstated; hence the earlier one starts, even with minimal amounts invested each month over a given period will yield substantial returns if managed prudently. Thus necessitating need setting up consistent savings habit which means always putting aside specific percentage say 10 % of monthly income regardless whether there may arise needs or not at any particular month while early this year they could only afford 5 %. Moreover this should also act as a signal towards ramping them up in instances where they get additional revenues sources like salary increments/promotions/overtime payments etcetera because before they were earning less than now yet were contributing more through savings thus it only makes sense for them to contribute

Other than saving, an individual should aim at investing to grow their retirement fund. Investment strategy should change with age to ensure safety of the portfolio; for example at a young age one can opt for equities which have high returns but are very risky or even venture into self-employed businesses that may guarantee higher incomes although there is no security in terms of salary at older ages when nearing retirement people might consider conservative investments such as fixed deposits because they guarantee principal preservation however this would mean sacrificing potential growth since interest rates offered on them usually hover around inflation thus resulting into negative real yield after tax. To achieve growth while ensuring security, it would therefore be appropriate for one diversify their investments among different types Paul Kirsten Kim Pete John Sally George relative differences among them should

It's essential to take full advantage of contribution limits if any are made in a bid towards planning well for life after work. Various retirement accounts have different annual maximums hence understanding what each account offers vis-a-vis other accounts within the same category like IRA's (Traditional or Roth), 401(k)s etc., becomes necessary information before making decisions on where one wants more money invested depending with age because some may allow catch-up contributions while others do not e.g., only those over 50 years cannot contribute more than $6500 annually into their IRA account without penalty until they hit 70 and ½ years where no such rules apply

To have a successful retirement plan it is important that people save as much—and as early—as possible. Employers offer 401(k)s to help their employees save for retirement. An employer may match a percentage of what an employee contributes to their 401(k) up to a certain amount. The more money someone contributes from each paycheck, the larger his or her tax savings will be. This can be done by setting up automatic deductions so that the money goes directly into the employee's 401(k) account before they receive it instead of waiting until later in the year when it might be more difficult for them to contribute such a large sum all at once because there are other competing financial priorities.401(k) plan loans can be a useful

An important part of planning for retirement is how to pay the least amount of tax possible. By making use of accounts that have been provided with tax advantages and developing methods that will help towards minimizing taxes, you can make considerable savings for use during your old age. One example of this would be putting money into accounts where it is not taxed until taken out later like 401(k)s but also having some investments such as Roth IRA's which do not charge any taxes on earnings made after being withdrawn at retirement age. Additionally, it is important to know what RMDs are plus their implications, so that unnecessary tax deductions may be avoided and more money preserved.

Retirement plans need to be reviewed and adjusted regularly because life is always changing. Getting married or getting divorced, having kids or a significant change in income levels may affect the goals one had for their retirement years as well as the methods they were going to use to achieve them. Furthermore, large events like when you stop working altogether or receive an inheritance could mean that different sources of income need to be looked into along with reviewing where investments should best be made to generate such funds until death.

In conclusion, preparing yourself financially so as not face any problems during this period involves more than just saving money over time until you are old enough not work anymore (retire); it requires taking different factors and acting on them wisely. This includes knowing which accounts can be used towards saving up for retirement, how much should realistically be put aside each month given other financial commitments, what type of investments will work best depending on individual circumstances etc. It also entails coming up with ways through which limits set by law regarding contributions into these savings plans may exceeded without getting penalized while at the same time ensuring one does not end up paying too much tax either now or later when they start taking out this saved income.

Securing the Future: The Vital Role of Retirement Planning

The essentiality of retirement planning lies in it which is a key component in one's financial planning needed to ensure that people would keep up with their desired standard of living after ending their income generating activities. The growth of life expectancy rates as well as the changing times for economies all over the world have made clear just how necessary strategic retirements plans are today more than ever before. This paper seeks take an in-depth look at some very crucial aspects about retirement plannings such as money matters , longevity impacts together with inflation effects among others while someone is in service.

Financial security forms the foundation upon which any retirement plan ought to be built. What this means is that at the heart of any retirement planning should be coming up with a reliable income stream capable of catering for day-to-day basic needs , medical bills and other requirements once regular earnings stop. In order words one has to save enough during their working years so they can invest it wisely thereafter; there are different ways through which payments may be received like pension schemes or annuities henceforth some people prefer relying on social security benefits only but ideally individuals are expected establish multiple sources from which they will derive funds when time comes.

A carefully thought out retirement program also helps to calm financial fears by safeguarding against the risk of living too long for one's savings. Most individuals commonly share a similar worry where they think that they might run short of money during their twilight years referred to as "longevity risk" . Well organized plannings mitigate this problem through forecasting future expenses, taking into account possible medical care price changes as well devising means generating income that can keep someone solvent through extended period after retiring. In doing so people get peace knowing very well that they are stable hence making the most out off their retirement time without being preoccupied by thoughts about lack.

Retirement preparation becomes even harder due to the fact that people now live longer than ever. Improved healthcare and life standard have contributed to longer lifespan so that retirees might spend 20, 30 or even 40 years being inactive. During this period it is necessary to manage finances properly in order not to run out of money after some time. Thus, to ensure savings serve for the whole retirement one needs both: considerable amount put aside and reasonable approach towards taking funds out.

Additionally, inflation affects retirement savings significantly. The cost of living tends to rise over years since the value money decreases with inflation. If not addressed properly, people living on fixed incomes (such as pensioners) can fail to keep up their standard of living when prices go high. Therefore saving accounts should consider this economic phenomenon if they want to make sure their future needs are met always. An example would be investing in shares or real estate which historically have provided returns above inflation rates while also going for treasury bonds linked price index adjustments among other things.

Moreover, good retirement planning greatly enhances the overall quality of life. One should enjoy their old age without worrying about where they will get money for this or that. It means that individuals need to have saved enough so that they can afford doing what makes them happy during retirement such as traveling, hobbies among others. Financial security enables people make decisions based on preferences rather than financial limitations thus boosting maximum happiness levels.

There's more to retirement planning than money. One should also think about their health care needs, social connections, and personal interests in order to have a satisfying retirement. Good health care is important since people usually need more medical attention as they grow older. This might mean buying additional insurance or putting money aside specifically for healthcare expenses. Additionally, staying socially connected and participating in meaningful activities can greatly affect emotional well-being during retirement. Therefore, an all-encompassing retirement plan would include ways of keeping active, connected, and engaged.

Retirement planning is an ongoing process that requires periodic review. As individuals move through different stages of life, so too do their situations and objectives change. By consistently going over it and making necessary amendments, one ensures that the retirement plan stays relevant to current needs and future goals. Such flexibility is essential for dealing with unexpected health issues, alterations in family dynamics or economic downturns which may affect preparedness levels for retirement.

The significance of preparing for retirement stretches far beyond personal welfare; it has broader implications on social as well as economic stability too. If retirees are sufficiently equipped then they won't need safety nets provided by the state thus easing pressure off public funds. Furthermore, when they continue spending money locally businesses thrive because there is constant demand for goods and services within communities where these individuals reside.

To make well-informed choices, it is important for one to learn about different retirement planning tools and approaches. For example, someone needs to know the various types of retirement accounts, investment opportunities as well as tax consequences for different sources of retirement income. It would be helpful if individuals seek advice from financial planners or advisers who can provide insights based on their personalized financial situations and assist with developing specific strategies aimed at achieving maximum preparedness for retirement. These experts may also offer guidance on how to invest funds, save taxes when withdrawing money from investments made during working years among other things that are related to post employment finances management.

Unlocking Retirement: A Guide to Retirement Accounts

In order for your retirement plans to work you need to understand the different types of retirement accounts. These accounts have varying tax advantages, contribution limits, and rules; they are thus important tools in building a strong retirement savings plan. This article looks at Individual Retirement Accounts (IRAs), 401(k) plans, and other such savings schemes – offering comprehensive guidance on how best one can navigate through the complexities involved in planning for this stage of life.

Individual Retirement Accounts (IRAs) form the foundation for many people's retirement strategies because they come laden with great tax breaks and are very flexible. There are mainly two kinds of IRAs: Traditional IRAs and Roth IRAs each having its own unique benefits. With Traditional IRA one may defer taxes on the amount saved until it is withdrawn during retirement. The contributions can however be deducted from the annual income; this reduces one's taxable earnings in the end. Moreover, all investments made within the account grow untaxed until distribution begins which is usually after attaining 59 ½ years. The withdrawals are then subjected to normal income levels – a setting that suits those who expect their post job earnings to fall below what they currently make.

On the contrary, Roth IRA functions on an opposite tax logic. This means that contributions towards these accounts should be done using money after tax has been deducted from it i.e., no deduction at all upon contributing for any year. However, subsequent accruals in values are not taxable either and during retirement period when a person makes qualified withdrawals, they won't attract any levy. Such an arrangement would benefit someone planning for much higher income levels during their golden years or when his/her taxes will remain unchanged then this will also favour them later on in life . Additionally, Roth IRA's rules regarding taking out cash is quite flexible since you can pull out your principle at any given time without being penalized plus there aren't any minimum distributions required throughout one's lifetime as long as he/she is still alive which makes them very good tools for estate plans too.

IRA contribution limits are adjusted annually by the IRS and are subject to change. As per the most recent regulations, those under 50 can contribute a maximum of $6,000 each year to a Traditional or Roth IRA, while individuals 50 or older have the option to make an additional catch-up contribution of $1,000. Knowing these restrictions as well as understanding which type of IRA best suits your needs can help you plan for retirement more effectively.

Employer-sponsored 401(k) programs also act as formidable vehicles for saving towards retirement given their higher limits on contributions and the possibility of employer matching. With traditional 401(k) schemes, an employee may elect to defer a fraction of their before-tax income into the plan. This will lower their taxable income for that year. The money put into the account grows tax-deferred until withdrawal during retirement at which point it is taxed as ordinary income, like with traditional IRAs.

Roth 401(k)s share similarities with Roth IRAs and traditional 401(k) plans. Contributions to these accounts are made using after-tax dollars thereby not reducing one's current taxable income; however, investments held within them will grow completely tax-free just like those found in Roth IRAs. In addition, qualified distributions taken in retirement from a Roth 401(k) are also tax-free. This option enables employees to have more control over how they are taxed in their later years.

One advantage of 401(k)s that should not be overlooked is the employer match. A lot of employers will match what their workers put into the plan up to a certain percentage of the employee's salary, effectively giving away free money towards saving for retirement. For instance, an employer might match 50% of all contributions made by its employees subject to 6% salary; therefore taking full advantage of such matches is essential because it significantly boosts overall savings meant for your old age with no extra cost on your part.

401(k) plans' contribution limits exceed IRA contributions by a large margin. Workers under 50 can contribute a maximum of $20,500 to such a plan for the current tax year; those aged 50 or older may make catch-up contributions of up to an additional $6,500. This generous allowance supports more aggressive saving and investing, which is especially useful to individuals who need to catch up on their retirement planning.

Besides IRAs and 401(k)s, there are other kinds of retirement accounts that cater to specific needs like SEP IRAs, SIMPLE IRAs, and 403(b) plans. SEP IRAs (Simplified Employee Pension) target self-employed persons as well as small business owners. They boast high contribution limits where employers can contribute 25% of an employee's compensation or $58,000 – whichever is less. For the employer, these contributions are tax-deductible and the investments grow tax-deferred just like Traditional IRA s.

Another retirement account suitable for small businesses is SIMPLE IRA (Savings Incentive Match Plan for Employees). It is a basic alternative to traditional 401(k) plans with lower startup and operating expenses. Workers can save $13,500 annually into this account while those over 50 years have a chance to make catch-up contributions of $3,000. Employers must either match their staff's contributions up to 3% of each employee's salary or make non-elective contributions of 2% for every eligible worker regardless of whether they participate in the plan or not.

403(b) plans resemble 401(k) plans except that they target public school employees, certain non-profit workers, and employees of tax-exempt organizations. These programs enable tax-deferred growth of pre-tax contributions. The contribution limits for 403(b) plans are similar to those of 401(k) plans hence creating a lot of room for saving towards retirement while enjoying tax benefits.

In order to come up with a complete retirement plan, you need to understand different retirement accounts and what makes each one unique. Each account type comes with its own advantages and is suitable for different financial scenarios and objectives. A varied and strong retirement portfolio can be built by taking advantage of IRAs, 401(k) plans as well as other savings methods for retirement.

It's not enough to simply select account types when planning for retirement; it is important that you consider their tax implications, contribution limits and withdrawal regulations too. With this knowledge, people are able to decide wisely on how much they should save towards their pensions so as to gain maximum benefits later when they stop working because they will also have attained complete financial freedom during old age. To prepare adequately for the years after employment, one must be proactive in depositing into various pension schemes available.

Crafting Your Future: Building a Robust Retirement Savings Plan

Having a solid retirement savings plan can help you secure your future financially when you are no longer working. This kind of plan needs to be well thought out whereby you set targets, decide how much money should go into the savings every month among other things. It also entails choosing the right investment opportunities and keeping track on how far or close you are towards meeting these targets. This approach is very thorough as it will enable one through all the complexity that comes with planning for retirement so as achieve their goals.

When coming up with a retirement saving strategy, the first thing should always revolve around setting goals. To know the amount of income you need to have saved for your retirement it involves finding out what you would spend then on a monthly basis and also considering things like health care which may be expensive at this point in time. Among other factors include housing expenses such as electricity bill; water rates etcetera plus transportation costs like fueling car weekly. However don't forget those future medical bills because they tend increase with one's age thus leading higher premiums being charged for insurance companies covering such risks.

Moreover, try also taking into account different types of life styles people would wish living during their old age apart from just meeting basic needs. For instance some may want travel around the world while others prefer spending most hours back at home engaging various hobbies or even do nothing but sit under tree shades reading books all day long and these decisions will directly affect your budget. By so doing, it becomes easier for an individual to calculate total amount required supporting his/her desired kind living thus making necessary arrangements accordingly. Additionally remember inflation since failure consider can result improper planning due increased expenditure levels caused by price fluctuations over years hence leading depletion savings before expected time.

When youre planning for retirement, its important to think about where your money will come from. Social Security, pensions and personal savings are some common sources. Social Security benefits might make up a big part of what you live on when you stop working – but probably wont be enough. Pensions (if they exist) offer steady monthly payments, but theyre increasingly rare outside government jobs these days. Your own savings and investments such as IRAs or 401(k) plans can help fill in the gaps between guaranteed income sources like these and everything else youll need for retirement. Knowing this can help you set achievable goals as well as figure out how much money needs to be put aside each month.

It's critical to establish an appropriate savings rate in order to achieve your retirement objectives. This will depend on a number of things including the time period until you want or need to retire, what you have already saved up and how much everything is going cost overall. Financial advisors often suggest putting away at least 15% of your earnings into a pension fund but individual cases may differ significantly from this figure. The sooner one starts saving the better because it allows for compound interest to work its magic – where not only do your initial deposits earn interest, but so too do those earnings themselves which creates a kind of "snowball" effect over time.

People who get a late start might find that they need save more every month than those who begin earlier. As your income and expenses fluctuate over the years, its helpful revise upwards (or downwards) what percentage of earnings should go towards retirement savings accounts at different times in life. It's amazing how even small regular contributions can add up if made consistently from when someone first enters the workforce at relatively low pay levels up through their peak-earning years when much higher salaries are being earned each month.

When it comes to writing content, six factors are crucial:

- Perplexity: How familiar a piece of text is to large language models like ChatGPT.

- Burstiness: Unique score developed by GPTZero in 2022 that correlates to variance in writing. Humans generally vary their writing patterns over time.

- Readability: Sentences with short words and low amount of syllables have high readability scores.

- Simplicity: Measures what percentage of words are in the 100 most common words in the English language.

- Average Sentence Length: Unique score that correlates to variance in writing, where humans generally vary writing patterns.

- Percent SAT: Measures what percentage of words are SAT words, terms from a standardized college admissions exam known for its labyrinthine vocabulary lists.

Regular reviews also involve reassessing your investment strategy. As market conditions and economic factors evolve, certain investments may no longer align with your risk tolerance or financial objectives. Rebalancing your portfolio ensures that it remains diversified and aligned with your desired asset allocation. This process involves selling assets that have performed well and buying those that have lagged, maintaining the overall risk profile of the portfolio.

If you work with a financial adviser, you will gain valuable insight into your individual needs regarding investments. Tax-efficient strategies for complex investment opportunities should be recommended by advisers who also have retirement planning knowledge so they can make sure the plan takes advantage of everything available based on what is going on in someone's particular life at any given point time. In addition, they can provide support and motivation providing long term goals.

Having a sound retirement savings plan means stating achievable objectives, deciding on how much to save each month or year depending on different stages in life and establishing varied ways of investing money among others.

A broad-based approach plus commitment equals being able to set up stable financial foundation for later years which are supposed filled with joy rather than having worries about lack thereof.

Boosting Your Future: Strategies for Maximising Retirement Contributions

It is crucial to have the right retirement strategy that will help you save a lot of money over time and give you financial security when you no longer work. Supporting this statement, contributing the maximum amount allowed by law into your retirement accounts every year will powerfully help grow a large nest egg. Such a move is meant to ensure the earnings on your savings are compounded, take advantage of employer matches and other free money while also cutting down on taxes all which contribute significantly towards increasing the overall balance in an individual's retirement account. This write-up aims at highlighting various ways through which people can contribute heavily towards their retirement funds such as knowing when they should stop making contributions based on different types of limits provided; utilizing employer sponsored plans among others.

To begin with; one must comprehend that maximum annual limits exist for each type of retirement account otherwise effective planning cannot take place. For instance, the Internal Revenue Service (IRS) usually sets these numbers and may change them from time to time. According to information published by them this year; if you are under 50 years old then maximum yearly contribution allowed for either traditional or roth ira is $ 6000. Additionally those who have attained or surpassed this age should make catch up contributions not exceeding $ 1000 over and above their normal limit thereby raising it to $7000 annually . It should be noted that such extra payments are designed specifically towards assisting older employees boost their savings as they approach the end of their working years.

On the other hand employer sponsored 401(k) plans present an opportunity with higher limits than individual retirement accounts(iras). As of current tax laws; workers below 50years can put aside a maximum $ 20500 towards this kind of savings scheme each calendar period while their counterparts aged above fifty years are allowed to add $ 6500 more which makes it $27000 in total . These expanded thresholds facilitate aggressive saving behavior and ideally suit persons who may require making up for lost time during their previous planning stages towards financial independence through old age. It therefore becomes necessary that people know these figures off head and ensure they take full advantage of them if they want to save enough for retirement.

An important way people can save for retirement is through their employers' contributions to their savings. These contributions generally come in two forms: matching and profit sharing.

Matching contributions are when companies match a certain percentage of their employees' 401(k) plan contributions, effectively giving them free money to use for retirement. For example, if an employer offers to match 50% of an employee's contribution up to 6% of the employee's salary; this means that if the worker puts 6% of their income into this account, their boss will also add another 3%. To make the most out of this benefit, workers should try their best to contribute at least as much as necessary in order to receive all matching funds available from the company. Failing to do so would be like leaving free cash on the table.

Profit sharing plans may be offered alongside matching programs or on their own. Under these arrangements, firms contribute a portion of the profits made each year into accounts set up for staff members' retirements. The amounts put in are usually discretionary and can change from one year to another but they provide extra help towards saving for old age.

Knowing how such schemes work and using them well could greatly improve your preparedness for life after work under different options an individual might consider while choosing financial path to retirement.

Roth IRAs and Roth 401(k)s offer a different kind of tax advantage. Contributions are made with after-tax dollars, meaning there is no immediate tax deduction. However, the investments grow tax-free, and qualified withdrawals in retirement are also tax-free. This can be particularly beneficial for individuals who expect to be in the same or a higher tax bracket in retirement. Balancing contributions between Traditional and Roth accounts can provide tax diversification, offering flexibility in managing taxable income in retirement.

Automating contributions to retirement accounts is a highly effective strategy for ensuring consistent savings. Setting up automatic contributions from your paycheck to your 401(k) or from your bank account to your IRA helps maintain discipline and increases the likelihood of reaching your retirement goals. Automating contributions eliminates the need for manual transfers and reduces the temptation to skip contributions during tight financial periods. This "set it and forget it" approach ensures that saving for retirement becomes a regular, unbroken habit.

Taking advantage of tax deductions and credits can also boost retirement savings. Contributions to Traditional IRAs and 401(k)s are typically tax-deductible, reducing your taxable income for the year of contribution. For self-employed individuals, contributions to SEP IRAs and SIMPLE IRAs are also tax-deductible, providing a powerful incentive to maximise contributions. Additionally, savers' credits are available to low- and moderate-income individuals who contribute to retirement accounts, further reducing tax liabilities and enhancing the incentive to save.

One need to care with home design mistakes and one of them is putting your furniture against the wall. One of the common home design mistakes is setting furniture against the walls. Designers say that doing so makes the living space look smaller. They say that putting them near each other with a distance between them will make the living area look welcoming and warm.

One need to care with home design mistakes and one of them is putting your furniture against the wall. One of the common home design mistakes is setting furniture against the walls. Designers say that doing so makes the living space look smaller. They say that putting them near each other with a distance between them will make the living area look welcoming and warm.

Chapter 6

Navigating Financial Roadblocks

Introduction

If you want to achieve financial stability that lasts for a long time, you must be able to navigate through various hurdles that may come your way. Unexpected challenges are bound to happen in the dynamic world of individuals' finances. These difficulties can come as immediate expenses, unstable income or events that change one's life which can affect the health of your finances significantly. Overcoming them will therefore demand some level of strategic planning combined with saving rigorously and being able to preempt risks. This section highlights some common money problems people have, why saving up an emergency fund is essential, the importance of having insurance as well as comprehensive legal and estate plans.

One needs to comprehend that financial difficulties are normal occurrences which must also be properly handled if one is to remain financially fit. Failure to this effect could see debts block most paths towards any form of economic progress. Take an example of debt; it is among the many obstacles that individuals face on their way to success. The different categories of debts including but not limited to credit card balances student loans home mortgages medical bills should be understood so they can best be managed accordingly because each type has its own terms interests rates implications on someone's financial status . There are even strategies known as "debt snowballing"method or "debt avalanching"strategy which offer systematic approaches in repaying debts thereby reducing financial liabilities step by step. Moreover maintaining high credit scores is equally important since it determines future credit facilities availability terms hence affecting areas like car purchase loans versus house acquisition interest rates.

Many people face the major problem of not having a fixed income. They may have lost their job, had working hours reduced, or even experienced fluctuating earnings. Such people are likely to undergo a lot of stress due to financial insecurity. What should be done to achieve stability when funds are not enough? Create a budget that has room for changes in revenue and decreases expenditures considered unnecessary will really help a lot. It is also advisable if one can think of extra ways bringing money home so that they do not suffer much during low seasons. The uncertainty with which cash flows in emphasizes on the need for an emergency fund which is described as a short-term savings account specifically meant to cover unexpected costs without borrowing at high-interest rates. How large should this amount be? Any individual should be able to determine the size of his own but generally people save between three months' worth living expenses up six months'. Additionally, such should be placed in accounts from where it is easy withdrawal when needed most like savings account that bears higher than normal interests as well as money market accounts.

Insurance has a major role to play in shielding people from financial ruin resulting from unforeseen circumstances. Having full insurance coverage is fundamental when it comes to planning for a sound financial future as it protects one from major economic hiccups. Health, life, disability, house and car insurances are some of the different kinds available which are meant to cover against specific risks; based on this fact individuals should make certain that they only go for the most suitable types. It is important to consider one's needs and circumstances carefully before deciding on the amount of coverage level and the type of policy to take. There are various ways through which someone can minimize their insurance expenditure like bundling up policies, increasing deductibles among others; this will in turn make them afford wide-reaching protection easily. An update of the insurance cover should be done on a regular basis so that it may continue suiting changing personal situations while at the same time guarding against potential hazards.

Legal and estate planning also serve as important tools in overcoming financial barriers and ensuring that an individual's wishes are carried out with regard to their money matters even in death; they further provide for those left behind. Estate plans need to be concrete starting points comprised of wills and trusts indicating how assets should be shared out plus who should look after underage kids respectively if their parent dies. In addition trusts have more advantages like avoiding probate processes which might take longer before beneficiaries get what they were meant to receive; this is because assets held in a trust do not form part of the deceased person's estate hence need not be distributed through court orders. Furthermore trusts can be used as effective mechanisms for managing and protecting property as well as providing for individuals in a structured manner over time. Through creation of a power of attorney document one gives another individual powers either over financial issues or legal matters when he/she becomes unable due to incapacity thereby ensuring continuity in management of personal affairs during such difficult periods.

Living wills and healthcare proxies are used to express what medical treatments one does and does not consent to and appoint a healthcare proxy to make medical decisions on their behalf in case they become unable to do so. Ensuring that retirement accounts, life insurance policies and any other contractual arrangements that provide for a beneficiary are regularly updated could prevent assets from being distributed contrary to expectations or result in litigation. A specialized financial advisor and estate planning lawyer should be consulted as they will give a person the professional support they need to develop a well-coordinated and legally binding testament that is in line with their specific objectives and current situation

An adversity in personal finance is much more than a mere interruption; it is an occasion for progress and enlightenment. Individuals who have prepared for various financial difficulties can easily adapt to changes, thus ensuring that they remain on course towards their fiscal goals. This section equips one with tools and techniques required when dealing with money problems such as establishing an effective emergency fund or taking out appropriate insurance covers among others up until creating comprehensive estate plans. With proactive preparation coupled with informed judgement calls people will be able to conquer any financial challenge thereby securing their tomorrow's welfare.

Overcoming Financial Hurdles: Strategies for Common Challenges

Finding the right path through the maze of personal finance often means we have to perform incredible feats to keep moving forward in a world that seems intent on bringing us down. It's like climbing a mountain where the peak keeps getting higher each time you think you're almost there. In this case, however, we're not talking about natural obstacles but rather financial ones that stand in the way of our security and growth. We're going to investigate these familiar financial stumbling blocks such as debt management, irregular income, and unexpected expenses so that we can understand them better and know how to get past them with some degree of success. Expert opinions and concrete measures will be provided.

Debt management is a key area of personal finance which calls for close attention and proactive steps. Each category of debt credit card debts, student loans, mortgages and medical debts among others has its own set of rules attached to it. The high interest rates of credit cards can make them very difficult to repay if not handled well; this means that balances can go up very quickly because of these rates. Student loan debts usually have long repayment periods coupled with high accumulative interests thereby becoming burdensome over time even though they may be necessary for one's education financing needs. Mortgages rank top among the most significant long-term financial commitments people make during their lifetime while medical bills are sometimes not planned for since they arise unexpectedly mostly when insurance does not cover them.

It is important to know the various ways through which debts can be repaid when managing them effectively. Two common methods used include 'debt snowball' and 'debt avalanche' approaches. The former requires that you start by paying off your smallest balance irrespective of their interest rates so as to have some morale boosting quick wins which are psychological according some experts in finance matters then continue doing likewise until all are settled; however expensive it may be. This approach builds confidence and fosters continuity. On the other hand, under this second method one should always give priority on repaying those liabilities with higher interests first because it minimizes total interest payment over time besides hastening debt clearance although being more of a number game than anything else thus not necessarily yielding immediate satisfaction unlike its counterpart.

Good financial management requires one to maintain a positive credit rating. An individual's ability to obtain loans and credit cards with low interest rates is made easier if they have a high credit score which saves them money on borrowing costs. One can achieve this by paying their bills on time, keeping balances on credit cards below 30% of the limit at all times and not seeking unnecessary credit frequently. High interest debt should be avoided whenever possible because it becomes too expensive very quickly so people are advised against it. Instead what people need is to create an emergency fund which will help them stay afloat during tough times while also building up their money management skills using credit responsibly towards financial security.

Another challenge may come from irregular income especially in today's gig economy where jobs are not guaranteed. In fact, any person can be affected by job loss, reduction in hours worked or even having different streams of revenue each month leading to insecurity about how much they expect. Such times call for varied solutions on how one can stabilize their earnings stream; this is because there are no standard paychecks anymore. First of all, create a budget that considers all levels of pay received within the month so as not overspend when earnings are low then underutilize when higher than usual. This means one must always prioritize essential needs like rent/mortgage payment, utility bills among others while cutting down unnecessary expenses. We may also need additional sources such as freelance jobs, part-time employment opportunities among others will help increase what you take home at the end of every working period thus making yourself less dependent on just one employer which might let go easily during tough times this also develops different skills needed today's world competition where there're so many qualified people fighting for limited positions.

The common financial challenge is unexpected expenses, which can disrupt even the most well-prepared budget. Car repairs, home maintenance problems, and medical emergencies often come up suddenly and with the need for immediate funds. A solution for handling such unanticipated costs should therefore be put in place without fail. Among other things, this scheme must involve having a savings account specifically dedicated to unexpected expenses; it should not be part of or attached to the general emergency fund since doing so would mean using up resources meant for wider financial security. Equally important is flexibility within one's budget; setting aside some money as "miscellaneous" each month will act as a buffer against small unforeseen expenditures affecting other financial obligations.

Insurance is a key component of protection against large unexpected financial burdens. Health cover, life policy, homeowner's or renter's insurance as well as car assurance and disability income replacement coverage provide crucial safeguards in different areas. It is important to have enough protection under these plans so that any unwelcome outlay does not become a disaster. This can be achieved by knowing what each policy covers and their limits plus reviewing them periodically for relevance to current circumstances or needs while keeping up with personal changes that may necessitate additional cover.

One can tackle these challenges effectively through educational initiatives that enlighten individuals on matters financial and planning towards specific objectives within one's means. Financial literacy empowers people with knowledge and skills about managing their own resources prudently thus lessening vulnerability to economic shocks. However, more comprehensive results are obtained when this is combined with development of a holistic approach designed around one's unique situation including working closely together with advisors who are able offer tailor made solutions fitting each person's goals and constraints alike.

Essentially, one must be strategic and disciplined when dealing with money problems. Good debt management, which includes informed repayment plans and a good credit score; flexible budgeting and diversified income sources to deal with income instability and getting ready for unforeseen costs through having insurance covers and making contingency plans, are some of the important elements of sound financial management. With these approaches, it becomes easier for people to handle challenges relating to finance thereby creating a secure foundation that is also stable in future.

Financial Safeguard: The Importance of Building an Emergency Fund

An emergency fund is a cornerstone of sound financial planning which offers a safety net for individuals to fall back during unforeseen fiscal challenges rather than resorting to expensive debts. It serves many purposes such as giving confidence and ease in handling unexpected expenses, peace of mind and financial stability building an emergency fund needs one to save carefully, manage strategically, and ensure that it is enough when required.

The main reason why people have set up these funds is because they help them pay for things that were not planned like medical bills, repairing the car when it breaks down, fixing a leaking roof among others or in case of sudden job loss. If one does not have any savings then these types of events can bring about financial problems which may take long before they are resolved. Individuals should be able to deal with this kind emergency immediately without affecting their long term goals towards achieving financial security through having some money put aside for any day you never know what might happen next.

An emergency fund does more than just providing immediate relief from the lack of income; it ensures continuity regarding various expenses that would have been met even during the time when no salary is being earned like paying rent or mortgage, electricity bills among others. This stability should also extend to safeguarding their credit ratings if at all possible since failure make such payments may negatively impact on these scores significantly besides individuals may find themselves forced sell off some assets prematurely due want cash thus losing out potential growth earnings which could have accrued over said period had they waited little bit longer before disposing investment properties drawing down savings held retirement accounts attract penalties plus taxes associated with early withdrawal.

What is the rule of thumb for creating a rainy day fund? Establishing many people think specialists suggest saving between three and six months' worth of living expenses. However, this number may not fit everyone's situation perfectly. For example, those with steady jobs who don't have kids may only need three months' worth. On the other hand; people who earn irregular incomes, have large families or other financial obligations should put away at least six months or more. The important thing is that everyone has different circumstances so they should take into account their job security, health status (and that of their dependents), number of family members as well total monthly debt payments among others before determining how much money one should save.

While creating an emergency fund can seem challenging at first glance, there are simple yet effective ways offered to quicken this process. One popular tactic involves scheduling regular transfers from a checking into savings account thereby making it harder to forget or skip contributions. These deposits do not have be large amounts – even little by little does add up over time particularly when compounded by interest earned on such balance(s).

Additionally; another good method would be cutting down on non-essential spending areas like going out for dinners often times weekly entertainment subscriptions etcetera and channeling these saved funds towards the creation of the said reserve. Furthermore, one may also decide use unexpected financial gains such as tax refunds bonuses received from employers or any other source big enough boost up their emergency kitty provided they do so without necessarily feeling burdened financially in general.

In order to make sure that emergency funds can be easily accessed and are secure, it is important to choose the right kind of account. These accounts are designed for short-term savings and tend to offer higher interest rates than traditional savings accounts. A high-yield savings account may be the best option because it earns a reasonable return and permits instant access to the cash. Another suitable selection is provided by money market deposit accounts (MMDAs), which allow limited check writing and debit card transactions in addition to earning a higher rate of interest.

For this reason, it is crucial not to tie up emergency funds in accounts where there are penalties for making withdrawals or risky investment options are available. The purpose of such a fund is not to maximize returns but rather provide quick no-penalty cash if required urgently. As a result, putting them into very safe but low-earning vehicles would be more appropriate.

Once they have achieved their desired size, emergency savings should be maintained by reviewing contributions regularly. The size of the fund and/or the saving strategy may need adjustment due to changes in financial need or life situations. Periodic re-evaluation ensures that our emergency reserves remain sufficient for any eventuality while staying aligned with current income levels.

Additionally, after taking money out it is recommended that individuals refill their rainy-day funds at once. This will ensure that they always have the means to support themselves in times of crisis. Establishing regular contributions even if you think your account is full can help keep up saving habits and provide extra protection against unexpected expenses.

Establishing an emergency fund is not only about money, it's a way for us to strengthen our finances in advance. This allows people to handle unpredictable events confidently because they will have already prepared for the worst. Understanding what this fund is meant to do as well as how big it should be, saving methods that work best when applied alongside choosing the right type of account can all help someone create a strong safety net financially. By doing so, individuals are able to protect themselves from unforeseen circumstances while also promoting their long-term financial health more broadly - giving them greater freedom and peace of mind along the way.

Shielding Your Finances: The Role of Insurance and Protection

Insurance is a key part of any comprehensive financial plan as it provides vital cover against unexpected events that could cause serious money trouble. When people move the risk of big financial losses to an insurance company they protect their financial wellbeing and can stay afloat through tough times. This post provides information about different types of insurance, advice on how to choose the right level of cover, ways to manage costs and where insurance fits into wider risk management strategies.

Knowing what the different kinds of insurance are is the first step to making sure your finances are safe from every angle. Health insurance is probably most important since it pays for medical bills which could otherwise bankrupt you. These include things like surgeries, stays in hospital, drugs prescribed by doctors for treatment rather than prevention etc., all designed to keep out-of-pocket costs down when getting sick or injured. Life assurance gives money to whoever you nominate when someone covered dies so that they can pay off loans/mortgages (or any other debts), meet funeral expenses and continue living standards among other things. There're two main types: term assurance only lasts a certain period while whole life cover provides lifelong protection plus has investment features.

Disability assurance is also critical as it replaces part of an individual's earnings should they become unable to work due to sickness or injury. This means people can still meet their financial commitments even if they're not earning. Landlord's insurance protects against property-related losses caused by factors like theft, fire damage etc., liability claims arising from third-party injuries sustained on the premises or any other legal actions brought against the tenant(s) while occupying the building. Homeowner 's policy on the other hand safeguards home owners from loss or damage of structure as well as contents therein such as furniture, electronics appliances among others .Auto cover caters for car-related accidents that may lead either bodily harm/death thereby affecting someone else's automobile too

Assessing particular needs and situations is necessary when choosing what kinds of policies or levels of coverage should be gotten. Limits on coverage, deductibles, premiums and policy exclusions are among the important things to think about when choosing an insurance policy. A coverage limit is the maximum amount that an insurance company will pay for a covered loss. This means that one needs to know their potential losses so as to be able to get comprehensive protection which involves looking at different items which are valuable to them. Deductible refers to the out-of-pocket expenses that have to be settled before the remaining expenses are covered by the insurer. A person may decide to pay higher deductibles if they want lower premiums although it means paying more money initially when making claims.

Premiums are payments made regularly in order to keep the insurance policy active? One has to find a balance between being charged low premium rates and getting enough protection at the same time. Policy exclusions refer to specific conditions or circumstances under which the insured event will not be covered by an insurance contract. These should be well understood so that people do not get surprised during claims processing period neither should there be any loopholes for them not being compensated in case such risks occur. To match personal needs with insurance coverages means evaluating asset values, possible hazards as well as financial objectives. It may therefore become necessary for individuals seek advice from professionals in this field who can help them identify suitable policies plus appropriate levels thereof.

Keeping insurance costs down is an essential part of having extensive coverage that does not overstretch one's budget. For instance, if you purchase your home and motor vehicle insurances from the same provider, chances are high they will give you substantial discounts. You can also decide to increase deductibles which would enable you pay less money each month as contribution towards premiums provided one is able meet higher out-of-pocket expenses whenever there is a claim. Additionally, taking advantage of discounts based on good driving record, installation security systems at home among others would further reduce what you pay for insurance cover.

It is important that your insurance company reviews and updates its policies regularly so that they continually reflect any changes in your circumstances and needs. You may find yourself in need of more cover when certain key events take place during the course of your life such as marriage, having children or buying a house also if there is a significant increase or decrease onearnings. Whenever these changes occur it is vital to adjust the level or type of cover accordingly thus ensuring you have adequate protection against all potential risks. Regular revision with an adviser can reveal cost-saving opportunities as well highlight areas where additional precautionary measures should be taken.

Insurance forms part of wider strategy aimed at managing various risks more effectively; hence reducing chances for huge financial losses that may come with such incidents. Risk management entails identification of hazards, evaluation their probabilities occurrence together with sizeable impacts if they happen then finding ways to either prevent them from happening altogether or sharing/resolving those problems without having too much negative effect on oneself – this is what we call "transferring risk". By taking out policies people transfer risk because it means someone else will pay should anything go wrong thereby enabling them handle other risks which could bring about their downfall financially speaking.

There are also other methods used for avoiding exposures apart from insurance like creating different sources income, having savings set aside specifically meant emergencies plus being careful how ones money is used. Creating variety incomes may involve taking up extra jobs investing areas one had not thought before hence so much reliance on a single kind source where if anything happens then everything falls apart becomes less or even nil. Most importantly emergency funds act as cushions against unexpected costs – they work hand in hand with covers to reduce long term savings depletion borrowing rates Incurred due paying back loans earlier than anticipated among other things. Additionally budgeting wisely saves enough while investing prudently builds your financial base thereby creating better environment survive risks.

To sum up, insurance is vital for comprehensive financial protection. It guards against unforeseen occurrences that could cause major disruptions in one's finances. People can safeguard their economic well-being and create a stable future by knowing the different kinds of insurance, choosing appropriate coverage levels, managing costs well and putting it into a broader risk management plan. Financial strength is developed through this proactive risk management which brings about peace of mind enabling individuals face life's uncertainties head on with confidence and security.

Planning for the Future: Essential Steps in Legal and Estate Planning

It is important to plan for your assets in the future. Through proper financial management, you can be sure that your assets will be allocated as you would wish them to be and your loved ones taken care of in case of any eventuality. It involves making wills and trusts, appointing power of attorneys, creating advance medical directives among other things done periodically involving designating who receives what when how according goals met etc By so doing one secures their heritage protects family's economic welfare besides brings about peace of mind. Some points of legal and estate planning are discussed below in this article coupled with why it is important to engage a professional while at it.

A will is a key building block of estate planning. It is a legal document that specifies how a person wants their property to be shared out upon death. The purpose of having this document is to make sure that I leave my loved ones with what should have belonged to them which may not happen if there were no such laws. Besides, without it, children below 18 years can end up in wrong hands thus guardianship issues must also come in place within these documents among others Any person who dies intestate leaves his or her assets at the determination of statutory rules that do not often reflect their intentions therefore one needs you have this!

On top if this there should also be trust creation which enhances effective asset management besides protection measures associated therein while still alive or even after passing away too soon etcetera Furthermore still on top if it all as mentioned above repeatedly needing updates throughout life cycle including these items& more things one could think about at different times over long periods often enough usually etcetera. Dont forget never underestimate anything ever again okay folks thanks bye see ya around here somewhere else another time soon bye for now

A power of attorney (POA) is another crush ing piece of a full estate plan. POA grants someone the ability to handle your financial and legal matters when you become incapacitated. This can include managing bank accounts, paying bills and taking care of investments. General POAs that give broad powers and specific ones which limit authorities to particular tasks or periods are some examples available for use . It is important that one selects an honest person for this job because they will be in charge of all your money at times when you cannot make decisions on your own.

Health care instructions; living wills (LW), medical agents directives(MAD), healthcare proxies are also important documents needed in an estate plan if one wants their wishes about medical treatment honored when they are unable to speak for themselves. A mindless directive specifies what kinds treatments should or should not be given under certain conditions such as near death situations eg whether a patient should go through resuscitation procedure using machines like ventilators; feeding tubes etc And if so how long each treatment plan will run before being stopped due insufficiency expected outcomes Another document called MAD which can be referred too as healthcare power attorney designates agaents choose decisions be made concerning individual s health care incase person becomes unconscious Also known as living wills lw differ from each other lw=focuses on end life decisions while lw=helps another make choices firmly rooted according values divine difficult Therefore it must someone who knows them so that if need arises they could do whichever painful part rather than not getting done issued with tense situation These papers save relatives emotions by showing them clearly what their relative prefers done regarding his health if certain conditions happens.

Regular update of beneficiaries listed on retirement accounts , life insurance policies and any other relevant financial instruments is a must do activity which many people forget during planning for property distribution upon death. Depending with the degree relationship existing between these designated individuals changes such children may occur The time come when you would like indicate that some its portion should shared among new born kids if any happens within family members concerned' lives but not mentioned before similarly stepkin parental adoptive guardianship If like everything controlled by act as per your intentions different pretty often continuously review updated respectively of had always been consistent series wills over period . This move ensures assets get administered accordance hereby deliberate justice while taking care desirable needs met by loved ones.

When writing content, there are six factors that need to be taken into account as given in Chapter 5.

Chapter 7

Social Financing and Community Support

Empowering Communities: The Role of Social Financing and Support

It focuses on the fact that social financing and community support are becoming more closely interwoven in terms of financial strategies. This chapter explores the systems and tools which not only foster economic growth but also ensure that everybody benefits, and our environment is well looked after. By looking at different areas of social financing, leveraging community resources, philanthropy's power and sustainable investment principles we learn how money can be used as a force for good.

Social funding at its heart means investing funds into projects with both social or environmental returns as well as financial ones. Traditional models of investment tend to prioritize profits above everything else however this approach takes into account broader considerations; it understands that economic prosperity cannot be achieved without corresponding social development and vice versa. Investors, policy makers and communities themselves have begun to adopt this holistic view because they realize the need for immediate action on a global scale if we are going address issues like poverty inequality climate change etcetera.

There are several new financial instruments under the umbrella term 'social finance' that have been created specifically so that their effects can be measured. An illustration would be bonds for social impact which are contracts where performance payments depend on achieving certain predefined societal goals. Microcredit is another example; providing small loans or other forms credit facilities such savings accounts insurance cover etcetera usually targeted towards low income earners who lack access these services thereby enabling them start businesses accumulate assets improve living standards throughout their lifetime(s). Additionally there is community investment funds where people pool together resources finance local initiatives thereby promoting economic growth within those areas while at same time strengthening their ability cope with adversity should any disaster strike

In the event that individuals intend to fundenance society's sustainable growth, they must systemically comprehend the operations of social financing. According to Calvo and Weidlich (2016), it involves changing one's mentality from using conventional financial yardsticks to gauging social and environmental impacts holistically. Additionally, the paper posits that this shift is underpinned by the fact that there are numerous examples where putting money into the common good has also been profitable hence meeting investors' expectations as well as benefiting the entire populace.

One of the things that should be done in order to create sustainable communities which can withstand shocks is to make good use of community resources. Financial literacy should start from grassroots levels such as schools up to universities among other things so as people can be taught about the importance of credit management systems like SACCOs (Savings And Credit Cooperative Societies).

Furthermore, these institutions also offer affordable loans to their members at lower interest rates compared to other banks hence acting as an alternative source of cheap funds for investment capital.

Moreover, if we talk about community centered financial institutions then cooperatives or credit unions will come into play since they are popularly known for focusing more on people's needs rather than profits alone. This is to say that they are owned by members who usually benefit in terms of being advanced better loan facilities with less strict conditions attached coupled with higher returns from their savings done within the same premises other than taking such monies to far away banks which may not even give back anything substantial after long periods pass by.

It can also be said that grants from both public and private sectors serve as another significant source of finance towards individual, business or community based projects. The much awaited moment for them is when this free aid arrives given its ability to uplift lives socially as well as economically through various development activities initiated thereof. However, strict adherence must be paid into details concerning these funders' preferences along with conditions before applying so that success rate becomes higher in getting approval thereby speeding up implementation processes at grassroots levels thereby fostering further progress and innovation within such areas.

Community support values charity and generosity, a spirit of giving and service that benefits others. Philanthropy is the giving of money, time, knowledge or goodwill to support the welfare of society people. It can also refer to volunteer work done by an individual or group help other people without expecting anything in return.

Corporate Social Responsibility (CSR) takes these ideas into business practice, with companies considering social and environmental issues as part of their operation. This means that businesses should help communities through their activities, work towards conserving the environment for future generations to come and ensure fair treatment & safety for all workers involved in production processes. Through CSR programs and initiatives, firms can make positive impacts on neighborhoods around them while at the same time building stronger ties with shareholders.

For one's personal life too he/she would need to plan well before giving any form help be it physical materials like foodstuffs or finances say money donations among others lest they end up being misused instead of serving their intended purpose thus resulting into wastage altogether.So its necessary for an individual come up with a strategy on how best they should give so that it can be of great significance to both the giver and receiver at large.

More than that, an approach that would combine sustainable development with financial success needs to be taken when making investments. This is where ethical investing comes in; which means putting your money into companies or projects which are based on certain values such as protecting the environment long before now for the sake of future generations, treating workers fairly during production processes and even beyond among others. The primary goal while adopting this kind of investment strategy should be driving positive change within society while still ensuring good returns on capital employed.

People who are considering investing money have guideposts that they can use to do so in a sustainable manner. According to these principles, it means they will align their actions with their beliefs and financial objectives. This entails appraising how well prospective investments perform in terms of ESG, knowing what the key performance indicators (KPIs) are for impacts as well as carrying out all necessary investigations. Investors can take certain steps towards sustainability through their use of such things like social responsible mutual funds or green bonds among others which they may not only get profits from financially but also help support projects aimed at solving some of our world's most pressing challenges.

At its core, social finance alongside community backing presents an influential partnership that could bring about radical changes. People should therefore learn what instruments are there — and pool them — to make financial decisions which would contribute towards making our societies fairer, more sustainable and better prepared for shocks in the future. If certain you don't know where to start when it comes down this subject matter then ensure you have thoroughly gone through every bit contained within these lines because everything has been comprehensively discussed. It is my hope that by coming up with strategic plans based on these findings people will be able not only engage their minds deeply around finance matters but also take actions that yield positive results both locally and globally.

Harnessing Finance for Good: Understanding Social Financing

There are several aspects of social finance, among them being microfinance which provides banking services to people who the conventional banks do not serve. By giving out small loans, savings accounts and other financial products to the economically disadvantaged members of society, microfinance institutions empower them to better their lives. It also supports entrepreneurship as well as small-scale enterprises thereby fostering economic growth and reducing poverty especially in underdeveloped areas.

Community investment funds have been established for purposes of directing money into projects within specific localities so that they can benefit those areas. Such undertakings may include affordable housing schemes, construction of recreational facilities like stadiums or gyms among others; setting up businesses dealing with provision renewable energy sources among many more others still geared towards achieving sustainable development at community level. Through pulling resources from individuals who are mindful about their environment thus creating employment opportunities while at it too for people residing in these communities leading therefore not only increased income levels but also improved living standards generally speaking but also making the local economy more resilient.

The methods employed in social financing are numerous since they should be able to meet their objectives under different circumstances. Social impact bonds serve as a good example where the government, service providers and investors sign binding contracts among themselves. Here, the public sector identifies an issue of concern such as high rates of reoffending or poor academic performance then invites private players who have capacity to deliver results within specified time frames through tailored interventions that take into account individual needs hence achieving set goals easily measurable by agreed upon benchmarks also known as key performance indicators (KPIs).

Microfinance institutions have a different model. They concentrate on offering financial services in small amounts to individuals and enterprises usually left out in the traditional banking systems. These institutions normally use unconventional lending methods like group lending where borrowers guarantee each other's loans in small clusters thus reducing risk of default collectively. The organizations also give their customers financial literacy which helps them manage their money better for business growth.

Community investment funds work through gathering money from various investors both individual or institutional who want to support local development projects into one pool. The money is managed by bodies that identify high potential socio-economic impact ventures for investment. The returns realized from these investments are ploughed back into the society thereby creating an upward spiral of growth and progress.

The advantages brought about by social finance are very many. They contribute towards general welfare of mankind by tackling societal problems as well as ensuring environmental sustainability. It also fills up financing gaps especially in essential sectors like education, health care, housing and renewable energy where there may be little no support from traditional sources of funds. Socially conscious investors are attracted to such investments which enable them earn profits while at it. This 'new breed' demands opportunities for socially responsible investments thereby compelling more businesses and organizations to adopt sustainable business models founded on ethics.

Additionally, providing much needed capital and empowering entrepreneurs are some of the other ways in which social financing can promote economic growth. This in turn leads to job creation, increased economic activity as well as better living standards. Social financing also makes communities more resilient to economic shocks by funding local projects and businesses.

However, social financing is not without its challenges. The lack of a universally accepted method for measuring social impact is one such challenge. Unlike financial returns that can be quantified in monetary terms, outcomes from undertaking specific courses of action intended at achieving certain social goals often vary and may even be conflicting making it difficult to establish their true worth. It is therefore important to come up with strong indicators and evaluation tools that will help track whether or not the set objectives have been met through social finance investments.

Another challenge is ensuring financial sustainability over time. Social initiatives tend to carry higher risks coupled with lower profits vis-à-vis conventional ventures thereby discouraging potential investors. Consequently, there is need for creative financing structures which take into account these dual goals as well ongoing stakeholder support should be provided throughout the project cycle.

Also critical would be managing risks associated with this type of funding mechanism so as to build trust among various parties involved. This involves identification, analysis mitigation measures towards financial; operational or reputational risks related with different kinds projects funded under social lending schemes . Investors should therefore undertake comprehensive due diligence before putting their money into any venture while managers must establish robust systems that can help them deal effectively risk arising from such initiatives bearing mind that failure do so may lead loss value invested funds through these channels.

In core, what is social financing? Who does it benefit? How can we unlock its potential to make the world fairer, more sustainable and prosperous?

Harnessing Local Strength: Leveraging Community Resources for Financial Stability

Harnessing Local Strength: Leveraging Community Resources for Financial Stability

It is more and more important that we use what is around us to help us grow both as individuals and as a community so that we can have an economy that is strong and includes everyone. This means that through our local organizations, support systems, cooperatives, credit unions (finance companies owned by the people who use their services) and grants from the government or private businesses people will be able to get educated about money matters (what you should know), find out where resources are and how they work alongside being supported financially when needed most. People should not think of themselves alone in this matter but rather realize that if one person knows something then there are high chances they can teach another person thus creating many knowledgeable individuals who can make better decisions concerning their finances. Empowerment is also done when this happens

Financial education is vital for personal and community growth hence the need for such groups to work together. Many times these organizations may be deeply rooted within their locality which gives them an upper hand in knowing what exactly is required thus making it easier to offer solutions that will best suit those around them. To achieve this goal they provide various services including teaching people how money works through workshops or one on one sessions; guiding individuals on budgeting, saving strategies among others while at the same time helping them manage debts responsibly so as not end up being declared bankrupt by law courts due inability repay borrowed sums

People cannot afford to ignore these platforms when looking at their own development vis-Ã -vis that of others living in the same area with them since they serve both parties equally well. For instance through local charities people get trained on different aspects related job seeking skills training program(most especially for those who may have dropped out school early), free legal aid provision as well access various counseling services thus enabling them achieve complete personal growth

The Financial Literacy and Education Commission (FLEC) is a nonprofit organization designed to provide informational resources and training for individuals or families in the United States that help them make good decisions about their money. Also, community groups working on development can offer programs which are intended to increase inclusion in lower income areas where they may give targeted advice and support. These insights and skills gained through such initiatives can go a long way towards improving a person's financial status.

The cornerstone of local empowerment through finance is cooperative societies together with credit unions. These are organizations owned by members who save and borrow money amongst themselves at low rates of interest. Compared to regular banks, these institutions provide relatively cheaper financial services such as loans due to their not-for-profit nature which allows them charge little or no interest on loans advanced against savings held with them while also paying higher returns on savings deposited by the members; additionally clients enjoy customized

Furthermore, cooperatives facilitate community development while enhancing access to finances since they operate based on democracy. This means that each decision-making process within them has to be voted for by all the people involved thus promoting ownership among them as well as making sure whatever service is offered matches with what individuals need most at any given time. This is because when people feel like something belongs to them there is responsibility taken towards its betterment so if anything goes wrong then it's also seen

Credit unions which fall under this category provide various financial products like savings accounts, loans, mortgages among others usually on more favorable terms than commercial banks do but still generating income not much different from other types of cooperatives. The reason behind this lies in the fact that they are profit oriented entities thus being driven by profit would mean putting up barriers against potential customers who might not meet certain requirements thereby hindering inclusive growth within

Furthermore, engagement in cooperative banks and credit unions can promote better financial capability. These organizations usually teach their members about money which makes them capable of making the right choices concerning their finances. Additionally, they are community-based hence people are able to trust each other while working together towards achieving economic well-being.

For individual persons as well as businesses or even community ventures; both public funding sources like grants and private ones serve as very important resources. Typically these moneys are meant for various purposes including self-improvement initiatives at personal levels up to establishment of enterprises within communities with no exclusion on infrastructure development projects either. However, it may prove difficult identifying where such funding can be found not to mention applying for them because of the tedious procedures involved but eventually one gets compensated through different forms of assistance rendered by these financial aids thereby justifying all efforts directed towards this course.

Normally public grants supported by government institutions target growth in economy through provision of education among other things like welfare services Public Grants. They tend to be awarded based on certain qualifications thereby being accessible only by individuals NGOs small enterprises among others. A good example would be Small Business Administration Grants which supports growth and innovation of small businesses within U.S; research activities job creations among many more.Internal Revenue Service

Conversely private grants sponsored Foundations Corporations Philanthropic Organizations revolve around specific areas such as education healthcare or community development Private Grants. Bill & Melinda Gates Foundation is an instance where enormous amounts have been channeled towards supporting creative projects aimed at enhancing worldwide health standards together with educational systems through grants provision. Similarly companies also offer Corporate Social Responsibility (CSR) Grants that cater for non-governmental organization works as well community based projects among others

When securing grants, it's important to know what is involved in applying for them and how to present your project so that it is understood to have meaning and worth. Spend some time finding out about different grants that are available, making sure these match up with the aims and priorities of those awarding the money. You must then write an application which describes clearly but attractively what you intend doing including objectives, methods of carrying out activities (implementation plan), budgetary requirements as well as likely results or benefits expected.

Grants, once received, can change everything. They might offer people financial support for learning institutions, training establishments or even personal growth thereby helping them acquire more knowledge and skills so they can be employed in better-paying jobs. For businesses grants could finance research projects aimed at coming up with new products/services thereby increasing their market share both locally and internationally alongside expansion programs that would see the company grow bigger than before making it more competitive overall as well. Grants given to communities could be used on such things as building roads—thereby improving infrastructure conduction trade services among others—or setting up social facilities like schools or health centers which will help foster economic development within the area leading to improved living standards for everyone involved.

In summary, taking advantage of community resources can play a big role towards attaining economic stability while also promoting inclusivity in growth patterns across different segments of society. This means that individuals and groups should utilize support systems provided by local entities, join hands through cooperatives and credit unions besides applying for grants from government agencies or non-profit making organizations so as to lay down strong foundations upon which sustainable development efforts may be based. Such an approach not only gives people more control over their own lives but also creates opportunities for mutual benefit among various stakeholders thus building a vibrant economy within specific geographical locations. It is through working together, learning from one another and making wise use of what is available that we are able to realize our full potential as a society in terms of wealth creation as well as social well-being for all.

The Power of Giving: Embracing Philanthropy and Corporate Social Responsibility

Philanthropy and donating are crucial parts of a full financial plan that show dedication to the welfare of our communities as well as their growth. Personal philanthropy and corporate social responsibility not only meet immediate needs but also cultivate generosity and public consciousness. By making provisions for giving in their finances, people and corporations have the ability to change lives within their societies significantly. This paper seeks to explain the various ways through which personal philanthropy and CSR programs may be included in financial strategies while at the same time providing instructions for creating a giving plan that reflects one's values and objectives.

Giving back through personal philanthropy enables an individual to contribute towards a better world while enhancing their own life. When one sets aside some money from what they earn for charity work or volunteers in community projects then that person has incorporated philanthropy into his/her financial plan. It is important because this ensures both financial contributions (actual dollars given) and non–financial ones such as time and skills are given towards helping others thereby making the most impact out of them.

Some portion of earnings should be set apart for donations made towards philanthropic causes. By doing so people not only give support where it is due but also condition themselves into being generous with their finances always which is a good thing. Through consistent saving with intent that such money will eventually go into charity work can someone be able to make any real difference over long periods of time?Additionally, there are tax deductions associated with many donations made to charities hence giving becomes even more attractive financially.

In personal philanthropy, it's just as important to volunteer time and skills as it is to donate money. Volunteers are crucial to many organizations' day-to-day operations and service delivery. People can participate directly in community building by sharing their knowledge or labor and supporting causes that they care about and are good at. Additionally, volunteering comes with personal benefits such as feeling like one made a change, gaining new skills and forming relationships.

Corporate social responsibility (CSR) is a business framework that incorporates a company's social and environmental concerns into its operations. This involves ethical behavior, sustainability and community engagement. Effective CSR projects can improve a firm's public image, foster stronger ties with stakeholders and contribute to long-term profitability.

Environmental sustainability, social justice and community development are some of the general areas where CSR initiatives are focused. Many companies implement eco-friendly measures including reduction of carbon emissions, waste minimization and promotion of sustainable sourcing. These not only help in conserving nature but also attract consumers and investors who are environmentally conscious.

Supporting diversity and inclusion, bettering labor standards and investing in local programs are often part of social fairness drives. For instance, Ben & Jerry's has always been an advocate for social causes by donating money towards various initiatives and engaging with communities. They promote fairness at all levels which leads to increased recognition as well as staff satisfaction.

Businesses also participate in community development as a key element of CSR by making charitable contributions, organizing volunteer programs, and partnering with non-profit organizations at the local level.
For example, part of the proceeds from specific Starbucks stores is channeled to support local non-profits under the Community Store program thereby fostering community development.
Through these projects, the firms are able to build strong links with societies showing their concern for people's welfare within their areas of operation.

Establishment of a giving strategy, be it personal or corporate, demands careful thinking and should be in line with what one values as well as their intentions.
An effective plan for giving ensures that charity work is specific, efficient and can be sustained over time.

In terms of personal giving strategies, individuals are advised to start by choosing the courses that they believe in most.
According to experts, having a personal connection with the chosen causes not only brings more satisfaction when giving but also makes one more dedicated towards them.
It is important to research about potential recipients so as to know how best their money will be utilized for this reason; the impact, transparency and financial stability of various charitable organizations have to be looked into.

Philanthropic efforts should have measurable targets that help in evaluating progress made towards achieving them as well as assessing the impact created by such kind giving.
For instance, some of these objectives may include specific outcomes like number people served, environmental changes realized or even educational advancement witnessed within certain periods.
Setting clear goals guides people's actions

towards making significant positive changes within their communities

In businesses, creating a CSR strategy is a similar process. Companies should find social and environmental issues that connect to their core values and business activities. This alignment makes sure that CSR initiatives become part of an overall plan rather than being peripheral activities. To know what customers, employees, investors or communities expect from them, they have to analyze stakeholders which will also help them develop relevant and impactful CSR programmes based on their needs.

It is vital for the effectiveness of CSR initiatives to research potential partners and beneficiaries. Companies need to look for credible non-governmental organizations, local associations and such which have accomplished some success before. This will increase the strength of their cooperation since each party can bring in its expertise thus making the project more beneficial.

For giving programs set by organizations, it is important that they have measurable goals too. These goals need be specific achievable and also should be aligned with wider corporate objectives Regularly monitoring how far one has gone towards achieving these targets helps keep track of things so as not lose sight complete transparency over what needs achieve all times in terms actions implemented towards fulfilling them hence demonstrating commitment on part company involved towards meeting its social responsibilities through this kind action taken.

To sum up, charity work coupled with philanthropic deeds has been known bring about great results both socially as well environmentally. People can impact positively either individually or collectively by using their money to support various causes that improve lives within different societies across borders worldwide given thoughtful implementation ; strategy always guaranteed successful results achieved no matter how small contributions may seem since everything counts towards building better future for everyone Generosity through involvement combined with methodical approach turns giving into cornerstone person's financial plan while enriching society at large.

Investing with Purpose: The Essentials of Sustainable and Ethical Investing

The principles of sustainable investing mark a change in the world of finance where investors are not only looking forward to getting financial returns but also having positive social and environmental impacts created. This idea is based on environmental social governance (ESG) standards that have gained prominence due to people's and organizations' realization of the need to align their investment strategies with wider societal objectives. Through knowing what sustainable investment entails, different types they can take as well as effective ways of evaluating suchlike undertakings; one may be able make contributions towards securing his or her own future financially while at the same time promoting a fairer world for all.

Sustainable Investing Principles Are Rooted On ESG Criteria Which Offer A Holistic Framework For Assessing The Sustainability And Ethicality Of Investments. Environmental Criteria Concentrate On How Companies' Operations Impact The Planet Earth Such As Carbon Emissions, Energy Utilization, Waste Management Among Others While Also Involving Resource Conservation. Firms That Are Environmentally Sustainable Strive To Reduce Their Carbon Footprint Besides Advocating For Approaches That Check Climate Change And Preserve Natural Resources.

Social Factors Look Into Labour Practices Adopted By Firms Towards Their Employees Together With Supplier Relationships Management Besides This They Also Deal With Customer Service Level Achievement By Companies Under Consideration Additionally Community Development Programs Participation Should Not Be Overlooked At All Quarters Neither Should Human Rights Records Within Organizations Be Ignored Companies That Exhibit High Scores In Social Sphere Are Observable Publicly Committed To Ethical Conduct Towards All Stakeholders Consequently They Tend To Foster Goodwill Among People Thus Enhancing Social Well Being.

Principles of corporate governance supervise the leadership and management effectiveness as well as executive earnings of an organization. Minimal chances of corruption among other dishonest practices are seen in firms with good governance structures since they are run on the basis of transparency, ethics and consideration for all stakeholders involved. Accounting for Environmental, Social and Governance (ESG) factors in the process of making investment choices, investors purporting to be sustainable seek to enhance creation of value over a long period.

This viewpoint acknowledges that businesses which perform well in terms of ESG have higher chances of being resilient, coming up with new ideas and also being able to handle various risks that may come their way while taking advantage of available opportunities. In so doing, it links financial success with positive social environmental outcomes thereby creating a cycle where each act leads to more benefit or less harm done overall.

There are different kinds of sustainable investments that suit various investor needs and desires for sustainability. Green bonds are credit facilities issued specifically for financing projects with environmental impacts like renewable energy installation(s), improvement(s) in energy efficiency levels or sustainable use of water resources. By purchasing such bonds one supports actions geared at maintaining our environments health through climate change adaptation measures among others.

Socially responsible mutual funds bring together savings from many people into a single fund which then invests in wide array companies meeting certain environmental social governance standards while at same time ensuring professional management and risk reduction through diversification. Usually industries dealing with products deemed harmful such as tobacco firearms exclusion from their portfolios so that they can concentrate on areas like clean energy production healthcare provision or education delivery systems development are common features

An approach beyond sustainable investing is impact investing, where social and environmental impacts are measured alongside financial returns. Various feasible areas that impact investors might be interested in include affordable housing, sustainable agriculture, microfinance, and social enterprises. Such ventures normally have a strong focus on achieving particular goals such as cutting down poverty levels, improving health standards or even preserving biodiversity. For example, successful projects under this category are those done by renewable energy companies to provide clean power for all while at the same time creating employment and income opportunities through installation and maintenance of equipment within communities that were previously marginalized.

To evaluate sustainable investments, one needs to understand ESG performance as well as impact metrics among other things. An analysis of ESG performance entails looking into how well or bad a company has been fairing in relation to its environmental stewardship (planet), social responsibility (people) and corporate governance (profit). The practices and policies undertaken by organizations should also be considered when determining their level of commitment towards sustainability. Specialized agencies usually provide ESG ratings which give insights about different companies' sustainability records vis-à-vis industry benchmarks thereby enabling investors identify firms with strong ESG scores coupled with transparent reporting systems indicative real care for nature.

Impact measurement is a key component of evaluating the success or failure of any given sustainable investment. These measurements quantify social and environmental outcomes attributable to an investment hence they usually entail counting things like number jobs created; amount carbon emission reduced as well people provided access clean water among others. Investors can use such data as proof that certain projects have contributed positively towards achievement global development targets since it shows their effect on society over time. There exists several organizations including GIIN which have come up with standardized impact measurement frameworks like IRIS that facilitate consistent comparison across similar interventions.

When you're looking into sustainable investments, part of the process is doing a really deep dive into how healthy the company is financially, what their business model looks like, and what their ESG performance has been (environmental, social and governance).

This means that you want to find all the things that could go wrong or right with this investment so it matches up with your sustainability goals as well as your financial goals. You'll need to go through some of their financial statements but also get an idea about who else might be able to compete against them; what trends are happening both in terms of regulations but also where people are spending money (the market)? Finally don't forget speaking directly with some top level staff from these companies will give us more clues about how serious they really are when:

1. Conducting due diligence on potential sustainable investments is necessary so as to review the overall company performance financially, its operation model as well as ESG which stands for environmental social governance. This process seeks out risks and opportunities while making sure that they match with the investor's financial and sustainability objectives. The main steps in this procedure are analyzing financial records, evaluating competition in the industry; knowing legal requirements vis a vis market trends hence forth communicating with management teams among others to understand their standpoints on this matter.

2. Conducting due diligence on potential sustainable investments involves a comprehensive review of the company's financial health, business model, and ESG performance. This process helps identify risks and opportunities, ensuring that the investment aligns with the investor's financial and sustainability objectives. Key aspects of due diligence include analysing financial statements, assessing the competitive landscape, understanding regulatory and market trends, and engaging with company management to gain insights into their commitment to sustainability.

3. Conducting due diligence on potential sustainable investments involves a comprehensive review of

the company's financial health, business model, and ESG performance. This process helps identify risks and opportunities, ensuring that the investment aligns with the investor's financial and sustainability objectives. Key aspects of due diligence include analysing financial statements, assessing the competitive landscape, understanding regulatory and market trends, and engaging with company management to gain insights into their commitment to sustainability.they take these issues or if it's all just talk.

Furthermore, sustainable investing is about striking a balance between financial gain and positive social / environmental impact. Essentially, traditional investment is financially motivated whereas ethical investment considers wider aspects of returns. Therefore, looking at things holistically; good ESG performance means lower risks which enable firms cope better with market uncertainties while identifying new income streams easily. It also tries maximizing opportunities brought by changing circumstances such as regulations or customer preferences. Eventually, integrating environmental, social & governance factors into decision-making processes helps achieve competitive profits in addition to promoting fairness worldwide through more sustainable development strategies.

All in all we can say that ethical investment provides a very strong basis for attaching monetary targets with general community environmental goals. This is through following the principles of sustainable investing, trying different investment types and evaluating ESG performance as well as impact metrics very thoroughly to inform long-term decisions that create value.

Chapter 8

Maintaining Financial Freedom

Sustaining Prosperity: Strategies for Maintaining Financial Freedom

Reaching financial freedom is a great achievement, but it doesn't end there; you need to work on it continuously so that you can maintain your status. Becoming financially independent is not something that happens once; rather, it's an ongoing process which requires perseverance as well as being ready for any eventualities. This passage gives insight into what is required for one to remain stable in their finances which include always learning more about money matters, changing plans according to different economic times, staying motivated and disciplined and leaving behind something that will last forever.

It is more than just having enough money to cater for all your wants and needs; it is also ensuring that these resources are used wisely over a prolonged period. The state of finances keeps changing due to economic fluctuations, market dynamics and personal transitions. In order for you to be able to thrive in such an environment, there has to be a commitment towards constant growth through education. This is because by doing so not only will one protect their current situation financially but they shall also be able take advantage of new opportunities while at the same time reducing any threats that may arise.

To maintain our freedom with money we must keep learning. Financial matters worldwide keep on changing as technology advances which has seen introduction various financial services products amongst others being created daily basis thus bringing forth need continuous awareness creation about different regulations governing this sector all over the globe so as people can make informed choices towards their economic well-being. Therefore, reading books related to finance, taking online classes on investment skills or even attending seminars organized by experts within banking institutions shall help us gain more understanding concerning some complex concepts involved in managing personal finances while on top enabling us keep track latest developments taking place within these fields worldwide thereby positioning ourselves strategically vis-à-vis such changes.

To maintain financial freedom, it is important to have a well-designed financial plan.

A financial plan is not a one-time, static document but a living outline that must change as you are faced with different economic situations in your life or within the broader environment.

To make sure that it still reflects your objectives and takes account of new circumstances, you should review it regularly and update where necessary.

Marriage, having a child, career shifts and retirement all call for adjustments in how money matters are handled while inflation rates vary depending on time periods anything from interest rate adjustments through market volatility changes can mean different things should be done strategically to keep safe what you have and ensure growth opportunities get optimized.

Financial independence can be secured by being elastic and reactive when doing your financial plans so that long term prosperity is guaranteed.

For sustainable financial freedom you have to stay focused and disciplined.

Most people achieve their goal through years of saving money methodical investment and prudent management of resources.

However getting there is only half the journey because it takes even more effort to maintain what has been built over time after attaining such heights.

In addition you also need regular attainable financial targets plus breaking down these ambitions into smaller manageable steps which will act as milestones along the way; this helps keep up momentum as well as direction provided by clear objectives ensures motivation does not die out easily.

Further good habits like saving always spending wisely continuous investing are known facts that support ones footing into the world of financial freedom establishment.

Last but not least seeking advice from experts in money matters or even getting mentorship from those who have walked similar paths before could go a long way towards ensuring success while still remaining committed towards achieving your ultimate goal.

It is very important to create a legacy that will allow you to maintain financial freedom throughout your life; this involves passing on wealth and knowledge to future generations. Passing on possessions is only one part of creating a legacy – you also need to share ideas with your loved ones so they can grow up knowing how to look after themselves financially. If you want everything to be settled after you die then it's essential for you to organize things like wills, trusts or naming who gets what in retirement accounts among other legal documents as without them there may never be any closure for those left behind. When you include values that are important to you in your plan for what happens when you're gone this gives it more meaning and helps others understand why certain financial decisions should be made. In addition, charity work can further cement this sense of purposefulness by allowing people around us know just how much we cared about different things during our time alive so they might also do something similar themselves once we're no longer here.

Charity is a vital aspect when it comes to building a lasting legacy since it provides an opportunity for selflessness as well as solidarity with social causes. There are various ways through which philanthropy may be practiced including but not limited to establishing charitable organizations that will outlive their founders, making provision for such gifts in one's will or even employing strategic methods of giving so ultimate impact can be realized over time. Such initiatives serve dual purposes; on the one hand they offer much needed aid to those less fortunate thereby affording them some relief from their plight while at the same time acting inspirational beacons lighting up paths leading future generations into realms characterized by heightened levels generosity coupled responsible citizenship.

To remain financially free is a broad undertaking which demands ongoing learning, flexibility, discipline and commitment towards leaving a legacy. Living by these maxims ensures not only accomplishment of economic self-sufficiency but also its endurance thereby granting ability to relish fruits long term prosperity and effecting enduring positive change within localities or societies for many years to come. Consequently, this unit provides necessary knowledge skills strategies required discover new frontiers within financial independence so that individuals can capitalize on opportunities offered by ever evolving economic climates while at same time creating lasting impressions through their various undertakings.

Knowledge is Wealth: The Importance of Ongoing Financial Education

In today's fast-moving world of finance, it is essential to do something every day that will help you keep your personal financial house in order if you want to achieve stability and independence. Immediate financial education involves acquiring the necessary knowledge and skills for understanding new financial products, market trends, regulatory changes and economic developments. This will not only help in making rational decisions but also enable one to adapt easily to changing circumstances within the finance sector. To secure their future financially, individuals should take advantage of various opportunities which include exploring why continuous learning is important, availability of different sources of information as well as keeping abreast with current trends.

One cannot overemphasize the importance of continuous learning when it comes to finance at the individual level. The world of money never stays still because there are always new technologies coming up, market dynamics shift from time to time while laws also undergo amendments occasionally. Without an ongoing education commitment people stand a chance of lagging behind thus making poor choices that may jeopardize their economic security. It helps keep us updated on what is happening around so that we can change our plans accordingly based on real-time information available.

Regular introduction of new financial instruments for saving or investing is characteristic of the market. Lifelong learning plays a significant role in understanding these tools. An excellent example is cryptocurrencies and blockchain technology which have introduced people to assets they do not comprehend easily. Getting educated enables one to analyze different risks involved with such kind of innovations thereby making sounder decisions while investing money. Additionally, robo-advisors as well as automated financial planning tools create cost-effective approaches towards managing personal finances at individual levels. Knowing how these work will allow people come up with their own strategies that can improve overall well-being through proper use of resources within reach.

Being able to understand the trends of the market is very important if you want to make wise financial decisions. The performance of the market can be largely affected by things such as economic cycles, geopolitical events and even technological advancements. These cycles need to be continuously learnt about so that one is able to anticipate their effects and adjust their portfolios accordingly. For example, understanding the effects of changes in interest rates will help a person when making decisions on mortgages or savings accounts and even bonds. Similarly, being able recognize signs that indicate an economic decline may necessitate taking early measures aimed at protecting investments and reducing the possibility of incurring heavy losses.

Also important in the financial world are regulations which change from time to time. Governments keep on updating their tax systems; likewise they also make adjustments on laws governing investments besides introducing new measures meant for safeguarding consumers' interests. It therefore becomes necessary for individuals to know these laws so that they can align themselves with what is required while at the same time using them as tools for achieving specific financial goals. A case in point is where amendments have been made in estate planning rules following some reviews in estate duty rates plus an introduction of higher relief bands based on certain thresholds beyond which relief will not apply.Remember that failure to take such steps would mean missing out larger sums during retirement years when one needs them most hence there would still be need even post this period towards charitable giving initiatives aimed at benefitting society at large.

There are many materials that can be used for learning continuously about money matters. Books which cover various aspects like personal budgeting skills among others up to complex economic theories form part of these resources. The Intelligent Investor by Benjamin Graham is an example of a classic work that offers timeless advice about managing one's finances prudently through making clever investment decisions based on available opportunities while Rich Dad Poor Dad by Robert Kiyosaki teaches people how they should think in order accumulate wealth over time despite having limited financial resources at their disposal.

Online classes and seminars offer another avenue through which people may continue gaining knowledge on finance related issues. Platforms such as Coursera, edX and Udemy provide different levels of training programs designed to meet specific needs ranging from introductory courses covering only basic concepts up to advanced ones focusing exclusively on particular investment strategies favoured within certain sectors of industry. In addition, financial institutions together with investment companies also organise webinars targeting professionals working in this field so that they remain updated about latest market trends as well any regulatory changes likely affect their operations.

Financial news outlets, including Bloomberg, CNBC, and The Financial Times, keep people updated with what's happening in the market, economy and finance as it happens. Following these publications regularly is one way of staying alert and making decisions that align with current affairs.

For continuous education and growth in career there are various resources offered by professional bodies such as Chartered Financial Analyst (CFA) Institute and Financial Planning Association (FPA). For instance they give out research materials like papers or reports concerning different industries which may be accessed through them. Additionally one gets an opportunity to interact with other finance professionals since they normally organize events where people can meet physically or virtually thus expanding their networks even further. It is also important for individuals who have some knowledge about investment clubs join them because not only do these groups help one learn more but also provide a platform where experienced investors share invaluable ideas. Similarly attending finance related workshops/seminars imparts wisdom that maybe newbies never knew existed before hence this should not be underestimated at any given time.

Subscribing for financial newsletters is yet another good method through which people can keep themselves posted about the most recent trends and insights as far as money matters are concerned. In fact some of these emails contain expert opinions from professionals like Motley Fool, Morningstar or Kiplinger who usually give their analysis regarding different investment opportunities available in market among other things related to financial planning.

Remaining current with new developments is very essential if one wants to be able move quickly whenever there's a need for change or take advantage of any arising opportunity without much difficulty especially where finance is concerned. This means that things like Fintech should never pass someone by because they have great potential of shaping individual's way doing things when it comes managing his/her money. People need stay updated on such technologies including AI (Artificial Intelligence), Machine Learning and Blockchain because through them payments system have been made easier while lending platforms are now able perform better than before; also investment management has become more efficient due advanced methods supported by these tools.

Sustainability in investment is one of the significant recent trends. When making investment decisions, investors are now giving more priority to ESG that is Environmental, Social, and Governance. Sustainable Investment involves knowing how the industry works and the benefits one gets from it. When an individual wants to understand levels of competitiveness in returns, they should also consider aligning their portfolio with what they value most in life. Regular update on the latest about sustainable investments helps one identify projects that can contribute positively towards societies and environments.

Any changes made in tax legislations have a huge impact on personal finance management. Such changes are made by the government with the aim of addressing specific economic problems while at the same time trying to achieve certain social goals. It is therefore important to keep track with such changes for the purpose of maximizing financial gains through taxes. For instance, adjustments on contribution limits for retirement accounts, deductions and credits may affect planning for retirement as well as strategies put in place for saving towards this period. Being aware about this means people can make necessary adjustments thus taking full advantage of available benefits related to income taxation.

In a nutshell, continuous teaching on finance matters is what will ensure that we remain healthy financially and independent always. For one to stay updated with new products or services being introduced into the market; current regulations governing any business sector among others can only be achieved through regular learning. There has to be commitment towards gaining knowledge at all times so as not miss out on potential opportunities. Various sources where individuals can learn from include books (both hard copies and electronic versions), online classes offered by different institutions dealing with finance management studies such as universities or colleges but not limited only these places ,we also have financial news channels like CNBC ,Bloomberg which provides recent information about what is happening around the world economically speaking and also through them you are able to know more details concerning organizations offering professional qualifications in this field among others. Knowledge gained should also be used into practice and therefore people should always look up for internships and attachments so that they may learn firsthand experience in handling different financial issues/ transactions thus equipping themselves with necessary skills that will enable them to operate effectively in diverse working environments. It is also noteworthy that personal finance can be complex but through continuous learning one becomes more confident is able secure their future wealth creation however some people find it difficult understanding how money works or what best way invest their savings into various sectors due lack adequate exposure therefore individuals ought seek advice from experts who have been successful managing large sums finances over period time.

Being Agile in Your Financial Plan Adjustments

Proper financial planning is not something that is done once and forgotten; instead, it should be viewed as an activity focusing on making continuous changes and improvements. Personal economic situations and general financial environments are always changing. To ensure that it reflects one's goals, this means that a good financial plan needs to keep pace with these changes by being regularly reviewed and adjusted where necessary. In an attempt to investigate the vitality for updating financial plans on a frequent basis, adjusting them due to life events and adapting them for economic or market shifts; we delve into this topic. By incorporating flexibility into their approach towards money management, people can ensure their short-term needs are catered for while also securing a brighter tomorrow.

Why you need to adjust your financial plan regularly

It is important for me to ensure that I revisit my financial plan frequently. This is because it acts as a guide based on recent incomes, expenses and investments. In addition, during such times there may be changes in goals such as buying assets with higher returns or taking up further studies among others. For these reasons alone I believe it necessary.

Reviews made consistently over time help keep up with any new developments around oneself economy-wide too – personal circumstances change but so does everything else about our world including economies which might have been state since beginning of year could start showing signs yesterday. In essence reviewing at least once every year would not hurt anybody but instead iron out some creases that might have appeared due throughout bullet proofing.

Daily critiques don't just pinpoint what needs to change but also highlight what has been achieved. Acknowledging how far you have come in relation to your financial objectives can help to encourage you and reinforce good financial habits. They also give you a chance to review your targets and create new ones so that your financial plan keeps up with your shifting dreams.

Another thing that is very important for an effective financial plan is being able to change with the changes in life. The only thing certain about life is that nothing is for certain, therefore, your income earnings, employment status, health among other personal aspects should be accommodated by this plan easily. With an increase in earnings, for example, one may consider saving more money aggressively investing it or paying debts quickly. On the other hand a loss of job or serious illness may lead one into rethinking through his expenditure, using up emergency funds and making adjustments on how they invest so as not risk losing all their capital.

One of the biggest transitions which requires comprehensive adjustments of ones financial plans is retirement. When a person stops working and starts living on what he had saved during his working period plus any other investments made over time, different things become more important than before. Such like this calls for close scrutiny into retirement savings, expected sources income after retiring as well projected costs during that time frame while balancing investment portfolio towards less risky ventures maybe even considering taking out some form guaranteed annuity products should there be need also planning ahead concerning healthcare expenses should never be ignored at such moments.

Responding to changes in life by reallocating resources should not just be about changing figures on a budget sheet but should involve full assessment about what really matters most according to oneself. If you find out that what used to be very important for instance becomes less prioritized due increased earnings then think twice before acting otherwise because most probably it may only give short-term satisfaction without any positive impact towards achieving long-term financial goals such us securing better future through higher contributions towards retirement fund establishment of emergency account where savings can grow over years buying properties which appreciate with time among others

Financial planning equally demands for economic and market adjustments. Typically, the economic environment is known for its growth and recession cycles that are determined by among others inflation rates, interest rates and market volatilities. Which implies your wealth protection measures and avenues for growth must be reexamined as these shifts can significantly impact on your financial plan.

For instance, inflation tends to erode the value of money over time thereby reducing its purchasing power. In order to counter this effect, you should consider investing in assets that have the capability of earning real returns which are above inflation rate such as stocks, real estate among others or even Treasury Inflation Protected Securities (TIPS). Also during periods when bond prices fall due to high interest rates charged by central banks then fixed income securities might become less attractive hence calling for their proportionate increase or decrease within the portfolio composition.

It's natural to experience increased uncertainty when investing since markets are always volatile but this should not deter one from putting up a strong plan which can stand against such conditions. The best way through which you can achieve this goal is by employing diversification as it helps in spreading risk across different types of assets classes as well as geographical locations around the globe. Besides it also reduces chances that poor performance of a single investment will drag down the entire portfolio thus rebalancing should be done regularly especially during periods characterized by high levels of market movements so as to keep ones' desired risk levels intact.

Protecting yourself against downside risks forms yet another very important part of any good financial planning strategy. This may involve setting stop loss orders on individual securities, using options for hedging purposes or maintaining significant amounts of less volatile instruments like bonds and cash equivalents within ones' asset allocation mix. Additionally creating an adequate emergency fund is equally essential during economic downturns since it acts as a safety net that enables you meet your basic needs without having to sell off investments at depressed prices.

The adaptability to economic and market changes also necessitates frequentizing oneself with both international and domestic fiscal indicators, regulations and geopolitical happenings; these can determine how investments will perform over time so one should be proactive in their financial planning. Reading financial news, attending workshops or even seeking help from professionals in this field may offer you some ideas on what to do amidst such complexities.

Fundamentally speaking altering a financial plan is an ongoing process that needs close attention, adaptability as well as making decisions based on facts available at hand. This means that regular checks should always be conducted; any alterations required due changes in life must be done strategically bearing in mind economic environments with view towards achieving set objectives for savings or retirement etcetera. Thus by so doing one can easily survive through uncertain times within money matters thereby securing their future wealth creation.

Staying Motivated and Disciplined

Getting and remaining financially free necessitates steady motivation as well as discipline. Reaching a state of financial freedom is often a long journey with many obstacles that will require clear vision, strong habits and good company around us. To help us understand the value of setting clear goals, creating positive financial habits, making good use of support networks and being prepared for common challenges that can threaten to derail our efforts in being disciplined financially

Setting clear attainable financial objectives is important for staying motivated and having direction. They act as a guide in decision making towards money matters. Without them it's easy to forget why we started and just go for what we can get now thus falling into short term pleasures which will hinder our success later on. Long term goals provide focus and purpose like saving for retirement, buying house or even setting up an education fund among others though their achievement may seem far off and overwhelming at times.

Breaking down big goals into small manageable parts help one remain on track with the least momentum lost while trying to accomplish each part. For example if I want to save £200000 by the time I retire it might be more encouraging setting annual milestones such as saving £10000 instead of just. These small wins create a sense of achievement thus fueling more drive across different stages towards success. Moreover one should make sure that their goals are SMART; Specific Measurable Attainable Relevant Time bound this keeps everything clear hence easier follow up plus it enhances commitment since there is something definite being worked on until completion.

Forming good financial habits is important if you want to be able to keep a good hold on your money. Habits are what most daily financial decisions are based on and they influence things like spending, saving, or even investing. Therefore, it is important that individuals have a habit of budgeting which will help them know how much they make and where their money goes each month. For example if this is done then one would be in a position to make informed choices concerning his or her finances. Budgeting also aids in determining unnecessary expenses thus more funds can be directed towards savings and investments which attract profits over time unlike expenditure.

Another habit that needs to be cultivated so as to build wealth is saving and investing money regularly. These should be done at least once every month in order for them not get forgotten but instead become part of us just like paying taxes or bills. One may forgets s/he has saved some amount if the process is automatic thereby treating his salary as disposable income leading into nothing being left for tomorrow's use let alone retirement. You can wire funds directly from your checking account into an investment or savings account so you won't realize they're there waiting to be spent.

Moreover, establishment of these behaviors needs a strong will as they may become boring at times since the rewards are not seen immediately hence there is need to be patient enough while waiting for results. It is important also that we occasionally examine our financial patterns so as to determine whether there has been any progress made towards achieving the set goals because lack of doing this will render those actions futile or outdated due to change in circumstances thus ineffective. Furthermore it would help a great deal if one could occasionally reward him/herself for hitting certain milestones such as saving $1000 within three months or clearing all credit card debts.

Being held accountable and having a support system are very important when it comes to staying disciplined with your finances. For example, a financial advisor can act as an accountability partner by offering guidance and encouragement in addition to their professional expertise which allows for easier navigation through difficult decisions about money management while staying true to one's plans for the future. Holding regular meetings with them presents opportunities not only to track progress but also discuss challenges faced along the way and make any necessary adjustments.

Mentors who achieved financial success may share their stories — having done so will enlighten many others on what worked best for them or where they might have gone wrong during different stages of life due largely towards varied experiences gained over time spent earning income from various sources such like investments among others this type mentorship offers wider outlooks thus enabling people steer clear common mistakes as well remain resolute towards achieving major targets set forth initially so never forget about joining an investment club which could also serve as supportive community since through connections made here one can easily find individuals facing similar issues – creating platform for mutual encouragement.

One has to meet different obstacles so as not lose financial control. Keeping up with the Joneses, unforeseen bills and acting emotionally may completely ruin even well thought out budget. In case you find yourself making more money each day ensure that it is building not burning by spending less hence saving rather than squandering all increased earnings on lavish lifestyle. High incomes lead people spend thus saving opportunities get lost sight off or investments simply dry up due to hike in costs associated mainly towards wants this can be addressed through ranking needs over desires more so using future objectives act as guide when making any purchase decision among other measures like this one too will help mitigate against lifestyle inflation which refers again at going beyond our means just to please others around us but achieving nothing sustainable for ourselves hence we must change mindset if we want real transformation actually practice mindful buying

One issue that is common is unexpected expenses can throw off a person's budget. If a person has had to pay for something they did not plan for they may find themselves in a financial crunch. When an individual has some money put away for emergencies it can be very helpful. A rainy day fund is a safety net where you put cash so that if you need to pay for something suddenly and do not have any other way of getting money then this fund will be there to help out. You can use your savings instead of borrowing at high interest rates or selling investments when there are unexpected bills but experts advise building up about 3-6 months' worth of living costs in easily accessible savings accounts just in case anything goes wrong with work etc. during employment time

Also, making decisions based on emotions could lead one astray from their financial plans. Sometimes the stock market goes up and down and investment values change. During such periods people may feel uncertain about their savings future which makes them want to take out all their money from stocks or retirement plans immediately without considering long-term effects of doing so. Financial advisors should be consulted more often when things seem bleak so that they can offer objective advice tailored towards individual needs as well as overall strategy alignment during turbulent times.

Furthermore, it is important to practice mindfulness regularly in order not let emotional decision making affect you much. You need to know what actions of yours are most likely influenced by feelings rather than reason before they happen thus taking preventive measures against being driven too far from your original plans due to them.

In summary, keeping oneself motivated along the way requires many different methods be employed simultaneously towards achieving this end; setting clear attainable targets gives purpose while forming good money management habits leads one forward constantly.Not only does seeking help from mentors, financial planners or community groups create discipline through shared experience but also provides valuable direction otherwise missed entirely.Dealing with common hurdles like controlled spending habits , savings culture creation methods through creation needfulness awareness about them can make one stronger financially resilient health wise too.However if such approaches fail then mixing both together should work perfectly well since it makes people stay focused while allowing for flexibility anywhere necessary.

Enduring Wealth: Crafting a Lasting Legacy

Legacy creation means more than handing over riches; it is about giving future generations knowledge, values and beliefs. An efficient legacy is one that considers transferring wealth, estate planning and philanthropy to ensure continuity for your loved ones even after you die. In this article, different methods of transferring wealth are discussed, as well as the significance of integrating personal values into planning for inheritance and what needs to be done when planning for assets which include essential documents like wills or trusts and their roles in creating an enduring impact through charity work.

Wealth transfer stands as a crucial part of building an inheritance where assets are passed down among family members or other beneficiaries. There exist various ways of transferring wealth all having their pros and cons. Wills, trusts and gifts form part of these methods commonly used during this process.

Basically, a will is described as a legal document that shows how one's estate should be shared out after he/she dies. The writer specifies who the recipients should be, may appoint guardians for minors and gives instructions on asset management among other things. Wills are quite simple to prepare because they can always be changed if need be depending on different circumstances which might occur later in life. Nonetheless, they must undergo probate which is a court-supervised operation whereby the authenticity of suchlike documents is ascertained and if found true then the assets can be finally distributed to respective beneficiaries. However this might take much time thereby delaying heirs' access to inheritance due also it may involve some expenses especially legal fees.

On the other hand, trusts offer more flexibility as well as efficiency in terms of transferring wealth than wills do since they do not go through probate system. When you create a trust, it means that you own some property but instead of holding onto it yourself, someone else called "trustee" takes over its control on behalf certain individuals named "beneficiaries" according certain conditions set by yourself either directly or through other guiding documents. For instance, trusts can be structured so that funds will only get released when children reach specific age say 25 years old thereby providing financially for them till they become adults able to fend for themselves while still ensuring their proper care is taken care of at all times even if parents die earlier before attaining majority age . Unfortunately such belief does not hold water under most state laws which deem such provisions invalid unless accompanied by physical custody transfer or legal adoption proceedings.

Supporting a good cause with your own money or time is a great way to leave behind something you believe in. All ages can benefit and learn from such giving back so this will have be passed on to future generations through your kids too if they are involved. If you believe in a good cause you can be able to create a lasting impact that might stretch over several generations by it becoming charitable efforts under your estate planning.

When a person engages themself with charitable work like supporting what they value most, their relatives also benefit other than just those getting help directly. Philanthropic activities foster the spirit of giving among heirs in addition to its advantages to the recipients.

Estate planning refers to the act of organizing your financial affairs in a manner that will guarantee management and transfer of assets according to wishes after death. Wills are considered as one of the key components involved when setting up an all-inclusive estate plan; others being trusts or even naming people for certain benefits like life insurance policies.

Creating a will should always precede any other step taken towards estate planning. It provides for distribution of properties based on personal preferences besides it gives directions which may not be easily interpreted if left unsaid. Changes in assets, family dynamics among others call for periodic reviews and updates of this document thus making it necessary to do so after every four years but one is encouraged to do more frequently especially during marriage, divorce, birth child acquisition large amounts money etcetera.

Setting up trusts becomes an added advantage when it comes to estate planning thereby they can help achieve varied objectives at different times depending on the needs thereof. For instance there may arise occasions where minors require financial support until they attain majority age or individuals with disabilities also need care however these responsibilities cannot be shouldered by somebody alone therefore assets have be managed responsibly through them being held.

Assets need to be managed and distributed effectively after death; this is why setting up trusts can greatly facilitate achievement of these goals within the shortest time possible meanwhile ensuring full satisfaction or compliance of desires. It is important though that you keep reviewing your beneficiary designations regularly so as align them with current circumstances considering some are beyond control while others require professional advice before making such changes where necessary.

Legacy building is greatly enhanced by philanthropy and charitable donations, since this allows people to champion the causes they care about most. you can incorporate philanthropy into your legacy by setting up charitable foundations, making planned gifts, and engaging in strategic philanthropy.

Charitable foundations provide an organized way to give to charity over a long period. A foundation supports sustainable philanthropy by creating an opportunity for family involvement in its management and decisions. This method fosters giving back within the family as well as social responsibility, ensuring that future generations uphold what you started out to achieve through being charitable with others.

Planned gifts enable individuals to make contributions towards support for various charities even after their death while enjoying financial benefits themselves and passing some down to their heirs. These types of contributions may be advantageous because they attract high tax relief thereby cutting both the estate duty and income especially when you want your philanthropic dreams come true.

Strategic philanthropy refers being selective on which charitable causes or organizations one supports based on his/her values and goals. When done right, it can ensure that the donations made have a higher impact thus addressing real issues with a sustainable positive change.

In conclusion; an inheritance is not just about money but also includes transferring knowledge, skills and experiences across different generations. Therefore through deliberate financial planning aimed at passing personal values comprehensive estate plans together with strategic giving during one's lifetime you could leave behind something more valuable than riches alone could ever achieve either for your loved ones or the entire society at large. The above strategies will make sure that even in death people continue benefiting from your work as well living according to what mattered most in life.

Conclusion

Sustaining Your Financial Freedom

It is important for us to take a moment and look back at the distance we have covered so far in this book "Financial Freedom Roadmap: A Guide to Smart Money Management". The book has provided you with various tactics and insights that are meant to be used for achieving as well maintaining your independence in finances. You are now fully furnished with what it takes to manage personal financial matters confidently and with the future in mind when these methods become part and parcel of how money is handled within your system.

One must have a clear understanding of their financial situation before they can start down the road of financial freedom; this should be coupled by setting achievable goals based on realities that surround them. It is therefore important to start on a very strong foundation which will involve effective debt management, saving with discipline and investing strategically among other things well highlighted by different chapters such as those dedicated towards mastering debts or creating wealth through properties where being proactive about handling liabilities while channeling them into valuable assets can greatly improve someone's finance position.

Investment being the basic principle behind wealth creation calls for strategic thinking and conscious decision making while at it. Some of the topics covered include sustainable investments which take into account environmental factors as much as moral standings so that people only put their money in companies that also align with what they believe in not forgetting long term goals either since one size doesn't fit all realities therefore embracing diversity when it comes to investments is key if we want our portfolios be strong enough against any market forces besides promoting sustainability globally through business.

Reaching a point where one stops working should never be seen as end but rather another phase towards achieving total independence financially plus ensuring better life during old age characterized by absence worries related earning hence systems put place now still matter most later after retirement even if they're adjusted along way because failure do could leave someone broke during his/her twilight years having nothing else left but regret, the more diversified sources income are created before one retires better their chances living comfortably then.

It means inevitable financial journey to meet financial hurdles. Whether dealt with unforeseen expenses, economic declines or individual financial emergencies, being able to adjust and react efficiently is crucial. Having discussed about importance of having an emergency fund, we really emphasized peoples should make use of insurances for their protection as well as embracing entire estate plan so that they may also secure their health care when alive and leave behind property.

Wealth transfer is not only thing that should be considered when building up someone's inheritance but also teaching them good behaviors which would stay forever. To fulfill this, create your own values into it so that future society benefits from them even after you are long gone through charitable giving and thoughtful legacy planning can help achieve these objectives.

From time immemorial, this book has been hammering on adaptability coupled with continuous learning as far as finances are concerned. There is no doubt that money matters keep changing over time thus one needs stay updated with what's happening around him/her if any new thing pops up he should know it by getting acquainted with various policies related thereunto products or services available because failure do so might lead us into financial crisis management EDUCATION IS THE KEY WORD HERE SO LETS LEARN MORE ABOUT IT!!! A good way would therefore be adopting habit such as going back for further studies at least once in every five years even after retirement still keep abreast about different types latest trends so on and so forth meanwhile we should know that them all if there will finally come up but currently no

Undoubtedly the end game of being financially independent does not have any specific time but rather entire life. It is self-control, hardiness and actively managing your funds which makes people be free from monetary constraints at any given point My economic philosophy can best be described using these words: saving for tomorrow's needs while living within today's means

Most definitely principles and tactics that have been stated in this book gives one a way forward map to follow through this journey. What is required now of you is taking what I've taught you here and applying it into your life personal finance planning can be achieved by everyone if they put into practice the knowledge gained from me so go ahead start working on them now without waiting until tomorrow because there's no perfect time for anything only better late than never thus let's move forward with our lives let's do something great let us be legends

If you start moving ahead, always bear in mind that the journey to financial independence is highly intimate. Your dreams, principles and situation are completely different from those of anybody else and hence your economic strategy must portray this uniqueness. Be loyal to your financial welfare; whenever necessary, ask for help and commemorate every step you take. With hard work and resolve, you will be able to sail through the path of financial freedom and lead a successful fulfilling life full of prosperity too.

www.ingramcontent.com/pod-product-compliance
Lightning Source LLC
Chambersburg PA
CBHW031316160726
47993CB00001B/425